A
Friar's Joy

~

Kevin Cronin ofm

A Friar's Joy

MAGIC MOMENTS

FROM REAL LIFE

Franciscan Friars of
the Province of the Most
Holy Name of Jesus

KEVIN M. CRONIN, OFM

EDITOR

CONTINUUM • NEW YORK

1996
The Continuum Publishing Company
370 Lexington Avenue
New York, NY 10017

Printed in the United States of America

Library of Congress Cataloging-in-Publication Data

A friar's joy: magic moments from real life / Franciscan Friars of
the Province of the Most Holy Name of Jesus; Kevin M. Cronin,
editor.
p.   cm.
ISBN 0-8264-0868-0 (alk. paper)
1. Franciscans—Spiritual life.   I. Cronin, Kevin.
II. Franciscans.   Province of the Most Holy Name.
BX3603.F75   1996
255'.3—dc20   96-32286
CIP

This work is dedicated to all those friars minor who have joyfully spread the good news before us for the past eight hundred years, and in whose brown robes and sandals we gladly stand, with particular dedication to those funny, creative, faith-filled friars minor of Holy Name Province. We also wish its dedication to reach all those who have honored us by allowing us to serve them, which has been our pleasure . . . a friar's joy.

"What else are the servants of God,
but God's minstrels,
Whose work is to lift up peoples' hearts
to spiritual joy,
that they might love God gladly."

St. Francis of Assissi

Contents

INTRODUCTION

Why Am I This Happy?

Did you ever have a moment when a voice inside your head said: "Do I realize how happy I am?" Quick! What am I feeling? Why? How did I get this way? What a surprise? Where did this come from? Gee, this is nice! How can I hold onto this? It's so unusual. Never mind, let me just feel it and enjoy it.

No, these moments do not come that often, do they? But when they do, they kind of give you hope, that maybe it's all worthwhile after all! Maybe my life has had some meaning. Maybe all that drudgery was meant to be a part of this peak moment. Maybe the perilous journey, the boredom of life, the deep pain, and often times in our culture, the unnecessary trivia and numbing experiences of continual superficiality, are all built-in instruments and equipment that can help us recognize the opposite and intense feeling of profound joy when a rare moment like that happens to make its most welcome appearance in the world of one's feelings.

The immediate thing I wish to do, as an extrovert, is to shout it from the mountaintops, and tell everybody I know. Perhaps it might bring some vicarious joy to someone else, some hope for their own journey, however dangerous or "in a rut" it may be. That perhaps there is something to look forward to in the midst of this "valley of tears." Sometimes these, what I like to call "peak experiences," enable me to go back down into the valley once again refreshed with some new hope, knowing that it was all part of the same mystery, the low as well as the high, as hard as that may be to either realize, or for me, to admit.

Can't We Stay?

Personally I like it here on this peak! "Can't we build a tent up here Jesus, and stay with you on this most recent Mt. Tabor?" And he says: "No, you can't stay, you must go back down, but this is a foretaste of your future. Imagine what I have prepared for you, when this will last forever? No eye has seen, nor ear heard, nor can you ever even imagine what I have prepared for you . . . something like you're feeling right now . . . but only it will last forever! I figured you needed something at this moment to empower you to want to work for your future glory, and to give you a reason to hope right now."

These gifts are precious moments to give the human experience some of its reasons for hope at the end of the second millennium. It's difficult to be a friar right now, but how very exciting! I wouldn't trade this moment or my history for any other! Yes, it's sometimes even embarrassing to be a Roman Catholic priest today, with all the scandals and broken vows. But I always console myself that the first hand-picked twelve weren't all that hot either! And look what the risen Easter victorious Jesus did through those ordinary twelve! Maybe he's still doing it through us.

Hopefully as you walk through these pages with us, you will walk through a timeless experience and recognize an endless repetitious pattern of how God keeps believing, hoping, and working through all of us, frail, limited, but most glorious creations made in the very image of Jesus.

Perhaps you may feel the connection to the age-old Franciscan tradition which has always been a breath of fresh air in the church, from the very start, when Francis was commissioned to "Rebuild, renew, repair my house, my church, which is falling into ruin." Perhaps you'll identify the very same spirit of Francis in the early followers whose little stories we revel in the classic *Fioretti* or *Little Flowers of St. Francis*. Perhaps you'll run into a modern-day Francis of Assisi, Anthony of Padua, Bonaventure, Friar Tuck, or even a Brother Juniper.

Our hope in sharing this with you is that you might be encouraged on your own journey, the inner one and the outer one, that you might begin to recognize your own peak moments, and then together we might give thanks "for the One who is Mighty has done great things for us and through us. Holy is that Name!" May God's Name be praised, now and forever and forever and ever. Amen.

How The Friar's Joy All Started

It was a fabulous fall foliage day, a fantastic visual festival for the eye! I was on my way down the Mass. Pike heading home from two of the more memorable weeks of my entire life, when, as I already mentioned, the words came into my consciousness: "Do I realize how happy I am?"

I had had the opportunity to conduct a "Francis Week" the first week of October 1995, at St. Francis of Assisi Parish in Medford, Massachusetts. First of all there is nothing or nobody more than Jesus himself that I love to talk about and share than the little poor man, Francis of Assisi.

A new pastor had just arrived in the parish, Fr. Brian McMahon, and they have the tradition of having their annual week of renewal for the feast of their patron, on October 4. This was a great opportunity to assist the transition of the new pastor, to help them all begin their time together spiritually in the spirit of St. Francis. This was not a formally "Franciscan" parish—that is, conducted by the friars—but it certainly was one in reality.

TWO BEST FRIENDS

The part that made this week so special was that two of my best friends from Boston, Susan and Tim Davis, had invited me and worked through all the details to get me there. They were the coordinators of the mission! What made this so special was that Susan was in my folk group in Boston, at St. Anthony's when I was stationed there right after being ordained in September 1974. I've known Susan since she was seventeen. Part of a fantastic group called Young Catholics, which gave me so much life. Susan sang and played guitar faithfully for over six years at our folk Mass. We sang and prayed together on Boston Common, Easter sunrise services on the Charles River, Christian coffee houses all over the Boston area.

She married Timmy, whom she met and fell in love with during the memorable blizzard of 1978. I was privileged to perform the ceremony at their wedding at St. Francis Church. I was chaplain on the *QE2* twice, both times her parents were on board for Caribbean cruises. I buried her father, and mourned with her the death of her mother. She and Timmy ran the testimonial for me when I left Boston. I have vacationed with them and their five children many summers in Hampton Beach. So you can see we were and still are tight. Now we were back working together!

The thrill of sharing St. Francis with her parish, and as she said the thrill of her sharing "little ol' me" with them, was sheer delight. What a marvelous week of blessing!

BAPTISMAL REUNION

The weekend after that I was to perform a baptism for another couple I married, Colleen Morley and Kenny Walsh. This was their second son. Br. Michael Harlan, ofm, and Lucille Stonis from our Young Catholics group were to be the godparents. What a joy to be with old friends at life's moments of importance! Colleen, Mike, and Lucille all had accompanied me to Rome and Assisi many years before on a pilgrimage, which is where they got to be such friends of Br. Michael. What a joy to spend time with Colleen and her oldest son of five, Conor, playing, joking, and teasing him as we walked around the famous Walden Pond.

Because my next mission was in Colleen's very parish, St. Bernard's on Monument Square in Concord, Massachusetts. And believe it or not, my very dear friend Fr. John Murray is the pastor there. John and I met on a pilgrimage to the Holy Land, conducted by Steve Doyle, ofm, almost fifteen years earlier. He, a Dominican friar on the pilgrimage, and I formed a priest support group which met regularly for a number of years in Boston.

STANDING OVATION

Fr. Daniel Lanahan, ofm, and I conducted this mission. I'd have to say that the time we priests spent together in church and in the rec room and dining room of the rectory will have an indelible mark in my memory. This was one of those missions where everything just seemed to click! The spirit flowed so spontaneously and powerfully. So much so, that when Fr. John was thanking us on the last night, the hundreds of people who came gave us the surprise gift of a standing ovation. We were just as happy to stand up and reciprocate! These staunch New Englanders stood and did hand gestures to playful Franciscan songs we had taught them. They responded to the spirit. I thought, "If that can happen here in Concord, it can happen anywhere." They also gave us one of our most generous collections!

BEST DAY OF MY LIFE

One home-bound woman whom I visited during that week said to me after I had prayed with her, shared Jesus in the Eucharist, and gave her the Blessing of the Sick: "Father, this is the best day of my life!" Hold on, there's even more!

FORMER ALTAR BOYS

What also happened at a wedding of a former altar boy adds to my story. Michael Luongo and his brother were two of my altar boys at the folk Mass during those eight years at St. Anthony's on Arch Street in Boston. Their father had left them and their other siblings to run off to California to "find himself." That left them to the sole care of their mother Marcy. Marcy was a young adult Catholic, also from Medford. She came to many of our events. But was ever faithful to bringing her sometimes most rowdy band of children every week to our folk Mass. I'm not sure if it was for a break for her, or just to let her kids be with some sense of community, which we certainly felt there in that auditorium in those days. Those children certainly tested us. I believe we treated them with some special care and patience as best we could.

TOO CUTE TO BE A PRIEST

Needless to say I was honored when Mike asked me to perform his wedding in Weymouth to a young woman who also remembered me from the TEC's held at the Cenacle. Her brother Tom De Sousa told me how "cute" Joanne used to say I was! Too cute to be a priest!

We had a great time seeing both families at the rehearsal dinner. Although I'd have to say there was lots of unease and tension all night. You see, Mike's estranged father had just come back from his life in California after all these years. For the first time he was expressing any concern at all for these his children. In other words, his second wife just dumped him and got rid of him. And he himself is in need and has been mooching, while seeing and staying with some of the children.

Forgive my feelings here, but I was doing my best to be a gentleman. I knew how awkward this was for all of them, and especially for Marcy. Everyone seemed to be trying to do the same. It was so uncomfortable to say the least. It felt like a scene in that fabulous new TV series "Touched by an Angel," before the angels come and work their wonders.

Anyway, here I am sitting at the dais with the wedding party, after many drinks and fun dances with Laurie, another Luongo, whom I just learned was a lawyer who works against priest pedophiles. However she has just quit because she saw how sinfully easy it was to get church money, with many doubtful and unprovable cases!

DADDY DEAREST

Guess who walks up to me and wants to talk? You got it, Daddy dearest! I sighed, held my breath and said a quiet prayer. I didn't want to get heavy or suddenly "priestly," if you catch my drift. Well, Mr. Luongo comes up to me and leans over the large main table, and says, "Father Kevin, for whatever this is worth, I want to thank you for all that you did for my children when they were growing up. I can see that they love you very much." That's all he said, and walked away. Wow! I just sat there with tears rolling down my red cheeks, humbled and grateful once again to be a friar and a priest.

DOESN'T GET BETTER

It doesn't get much better than that! Who in this life ever gets the chance to feel that they really made some difference? What a fulfilling and yet humbling feeling. I was only trying to be a good priest . . . and it worked!

Now can you see, that after sharing some of the experiences of those two weeks in my Christmas letter, that one wonderful little lovely lady, Betty Newton of Pompton Lakes, New Jersey, said to me: "Father Kevin, thank you for sharing all that with us! We need to hear that stuff! We need to hear some good news about our friars and priests! It gives us hope!"

And so, here we are . . . sharing a friar's joy! It will be a joy for us to share these real-life moments in our lives when God has used us simply or powerfully as instruments. It will be a joy to share those tiny wisdom insights we learned when trying to serve faithfully. Perhaps you will catch some of that joy and perhaps have more hope. That would be our delight, as we all wait . . . in joyful hope!

NEVER MET A FRIAR

Someone once told me that: "I never met a Franciscan friar that I didn't feel better after I did." I hope you feel better after you meet us real-live twentieth-century sons and brothers of Francis of Assisi, Anthony of Padua, Juniper Serra, Bonaventure, Bernadine of Siena, Friar Tuck, and Brother Juniper. We hope you get some "holy friar broth for your soul," as you read through this modern-day *Fioretti* or *Little Flowers of St. Francis!*

God of My Gladness and Joy

I will go in to the altar of God, the God of my
gladness and joy.
Psalm 43:4

Tavern Owner's Son

Besides being a Depression era "Baby Boomer" from Brooklyn, I was the twelfth child of tavern owner Dan Lanahan of County Cork, Ireland, and Margaret nee Sheehan. Being a tavern owner's son had profound influence on my life and ministry as a friar.

Before Welfare, the tavern (or bar) played a major social role in a neighborhood. When someone lost a job or had a fire in the home or a kid in trouble with the law, one of the first persons to go to for help was the tavern owner. Often my father passed the word around that Jimmy Murphy needed a job, or the Dennihey's needed furniture to replace what was destroyed in the fire. Off-duty policemen were approached cautiously by Pop Lanahan to do what they could for some Billie Boy in trouble. I could not tell you how many Saturday-night benefits he ran to help the poor, and only God knows, how many rents he helped to pay.

More than a watering place, but never less, it was a center for networking and an institution of compassion. A well-respected bartender rivaled the parish priest in being a good "confessor" with his excellent listening skills. He often surpassed the local clergy as an effective minister of Good News because he was by necessity and choice immersed in the messiness of the human condition. Growing up in this milieu and being at home in it influenced me profoundly as a person called to be a caring human being willing to pay attention to a great variety of people with challenging behavior patterns. Peace did not always reign in the bar. Early in life I learned that it is better to head things off at the pass or, in other words, to prevent a fight than to stop one. In fact, if it is too late to stop it, your best bet is to encourage them to move the event outdoors!

Throughout thirty plus years of priestly ministry, this tavern owner's son has tried to listen compassionately to the people God has sent into his life. Modeling myself on the good bartender (read Pop Lanahan), I tried to understand rather than be understood.

Too many of my "customers" will immediately shout out, "You didn't always listen or respond with tender loving care!" No, I did not. However, when I did listen long and lovingly with reverence, I cannot describe the incredible joy in being an eyewitness to the awesome mystery of God's grace moving some-one to discover the terrible beauty and power of their goodness and their freedom to love and to be loved. The joy of contemplating the Creator's artistry in the radiant beauty of another person's heart and soul still leaves me lost in wonder.

Although my concerns were centered upon people's spiritual welfare, my heart has always remained essentially the heart of a tavern owner's son—the heart of a compassionate listener.

To Pop and all the Lanahan customers I gratefully lift a toast in their honor. Cheers!

friar Daniel

* * *

Good Roots

It was my good fortune to grow up on a farm in upstate New York. I'm sure that those who were reared in a city or large town might feel equally blessed. But I never experienced city living until well into my mature years and never adapted well to it.

My childhood memories include the sight of autumn sunlight filtering through red and yellow leaves, the smell of wet earth after a summer rain, the buzz of bees harvesting pollen from the flowers in the pasture, the taste of a northern spy apple.

Sense memories, to be sure, but sense memories not of people and city activity, but of the cycle and rhythm of nature.

The marvels of nature played a large part in my childhood and have continued to energize me. Two factors aided me in an appreciation of the natural world around me. One, aloneness. Raised on a farm, there were few opportunities for playmates, especially during the summer vacations. Too, I was the middle child. My brother was almost four years older than I, and my sister six years my junior. For entertainment I fell back on what was around me; the farm, the fields, and woods.

Secondly, my father. He had grown up on the same farm and knew every part of it. He could tell the track of a raccoon from that of a muskrat in the mud of the brook that ran through our pasture. He knew a robin's egg from a blue bird's. When it would snow, he knew how to catch the weasel ravaging our chickens. The knowledge of wild things, the wonder, the respect for nature, he tried to pass on to me.

INTERIOR LIFE

Time spent by myself in the autumn woods or bringing down the cows on a hot summer afternoon prepared me for an interior life I might never have otherwise explored. Any young life is full of mystery, but I expect that on a farm the mysteries are closer to hand and even more palpable. The mystery of life as a cow drops a calf or a chick breaks through the shell of the egg, the mystery of growth as kernels of corn become blades, then stalks; the mystery of death as the young calf is sold to a butcher, the chicken killed for a Sunday meal, the corn harvested and put in the silo. The cycle, whether of seed or animal or human being, pulses inexorably year upon year. And under that pulse did I not perceive somehow a guiding power that governed and sustained it all?

DOWN THE HIGHWAY

Down the highway, the second farm, there lived my second cousins Herb and Florence. They were both elderly, beyond the years to do the hard physical work of planting and harvesting. Herb raised prize bulls for breeding and kept an ice house, both of which brought in a small income. And Florence took in tourists, offering them a clean and comfortable room at night, breakfast in the morning. Taking in tourists was a usual way of gaining extra income in those days for people lucky enough to live beside a busy road.

Florence was small and plump, white-haired and red-cheeked, a constant worker at cleaning the house, doing the bedding and baking. Her house always smelled of freshly baked bread, cake, or pie, and was eager to part with a slice of her bread with home-churned butter on it, sprinkled with brown sugar.

Not able to have children, they had adopted a girl. Much older than I, I never met her because, my folks told me, she had not "turned out well and run away to the city." That was a sadness in Florence's life; but never did she complain. No, although always engrossed in some task, she had time for us children when we would drop in on her. She was, in her own way, one of my teachers. She exemplified for me the virtue of work, of joyful and patient endurance under hardship.

friar Roderic

* * *

Love Measured in Gallons

At a recent gathering of men for prayer one Saturday morning, the question was asked, "How does one experience God?" One of the men spoke of good preaching, while another suggested personal testimony. A man in the back row, who looked to be in his mid-fifties, expressed his feelings of how he had come to experience God. He said that he grew up in a small town in New Jersey, which could easily be identified with the fictional town of Mayberry in the classic *Andy Griffith Show*. Since we were just one week into the Easter season, this gentleman began to reminisce on how his mom made those traditional buns on Good Friday and how the aroma filled the whole house. He also began to speak about his mom. Though he had been away from the Church for many years as a young adult, he felt that his experience of God had come to him through his mom.

SEEING FOR THE FIRST TIME

He recalled visiting his hometown a few years ago and stopping in to pray at his parish church. His prayer to God went something like this: "You were here all the while, Lord?!" As he shared with us, I recalled to mind the quote of T. S. Eliot: "After all of our exploring is to arrive where we started and to see the place for the first time."

I wish I knew why it takes so many times, so many years for this Franciscan, to see what was obviously in front of me from the very beginning. But do you ever feel, in light of some of the personalities in the Scriptures, that maybe we are not so alone? It took Peter and many of those early disciples years before they recognized the depth of Jesus' message to them. If one examines the life of any saint, it was very much the same way.

ALWAYS THERE

Maybe that is why someone like Francis of Assisi has had so much appeal. Even towards the end of his life, there is still so much need for conversion. In his last will and testament one gets a sense that Francis has become aware that it was in the leper and in the brothers that there was a God who was always already there in his life.

Two years ago I was struck with the awareness of God through the life of my mother. My family had decided to have a surprise seventieth birthday party for mom in late December, about a week after her birthday. Since I was up to New York anyway for the Christmas holidays, my mom was none the wiser about the upcoming event that was to be held in a few days. Often at the end of the day, I would pause and wonder what I would say at the family Mass that we were planning.

AS MOM SHOPPED

One evening mom invited me to go downtown with her to pick up a gift for my niece Rayann who would be celebrating her tenth birthday. Mom had been meaning to do this for days but it was only now, at this late hour, that she found the time. As mom shopped I was touched by her comments as she carefully examined each item that she picked up. "This top will go with Rayann's brown hair. This color will accentuate her beautiful smile, . . . this bracelet her delicate features." It occurred to me that mom wasn't shopping for just a ten-year old, she was shopping for her granddaughter whom she loves and knows very well. I thought to myself later on, that mom has stood in this one department store alone, to buy gifts, not just for her husband, not just for her seven kids, not just for her eighteen grandchildren, but for so many other relatives and friends. And always there is the love, the interest, the care that she demonstrated when shopping for Rayann.

PICKING UP

It all kind of made sense to me then, as I looked for a chair to sit down, why mom's back often hurts. Standing for any stretch of time can always put a strain on your back. Be it picking up gifts, picking up babies, picking up laundry, picking up dishes, or picking up groceries, Mom's aching back has been at it for over fifty years. It's all quite amazing to me now, because as I reflect, I see that in this labor of love, mom has always maintained that capacity to pick up a sagging spirit, to lift up a discouraged heart. I see now that I have experienced God in a profound way through my mom. It does seem like it takes me so many years before I finally see the way things are . . . before I see the nearness of God.

GALLONS OF LOVE

The next day as I reflected on the wedding feast of Cana, the gospel that would be proclaimed at the family Mass, the six stone jars filled with water and transformed into wine by Jesus, took on new meaning. If love could be measured in gallons, then my mother has spent figuratively gallons and gallons of love, a whole watershed of love for the sake of others. So often we in the family were the stone cold empty jars.

It is one thing to fill those "jars" with water . . . putting food in your body and clothes on your back or buying someone a gift, but it is totally another to do those actions with love. That is what is so beautiful about the wedding feast of Cana. Jesus cared about this young couple's possible embarrassment.

DIVINE INFUSION

What makes the wedding feast spiritual and divine is the infusion of God's love. Jesus took a very common aspect of our broken humanity and he divinized it with love.

Mom's love is a reflection of God's love. Over the years mom has taken so many of the broken aspects of being human, of being a family, and she has infused them with love. One rarely notices this divine love when he or she is a kid. One often misses it, in the day-to-day of one's present life, but like the sun that shines and the air we breathe, the divine love of God has been there for me and it is one significant way that I have come to know the transforming love of God.

THE BEST

It is a love that always gives the best. Whoever wrote the Polish proverb: "That even the cook who cooks a fly saves the breast for himself" didn't know my mom. She always, to this day, seems to save the best and choicest for others.

At family get-togethers when the house is often full, it's not uncommon for my family, like others, to plunge the inner depths, to theologize and philosophize about life and current events. It is also not uncommon for us to disagree. But underlying those gatherings, there seems to be a real love, a real sense of how we care and serve each other.

It doesn't take a rocket scientist to figure where we learned that type of committed love. To some extent, I guess that we learn through preaching and personal testimonies, but really, I believe we learn it best from those first places where we shared the community of God's love.

For many people in our world today, some have not experienced that community until they went to school and met a caring teacher, joined a support group/religious community, got married or found a lasting friend. But for many, those real signs of love came from the day they were born. We don't always see it but it is there. It is celebrated and proclaimed at every Eucharist and it is from there that Jesus, the source of our love, fills us with God's love to serve others.

THANKS MOM

For me the first dispenser of that love, before any priest ever poured any water over my head or before I really ever understood the power of the Eucharist was my mom. And so I want to say, "Thanks Mom!" It is appreciated beyond all telling.

friar Thomas

* * *

Stop Laughing at My Behind

It all started in my senior year in high school, (St. Mary's, Rutherford, New Jersey) when the class made a mission/retreat and the talk on vocations hit me between the eyes. I fought it for a while but figured I'd better go and see what this is all about. In the seminary I didn't come with a black suit because I wasn't sure I was staying. In the summer I also reestablished a relationship with "Pinky" Rogers, a girl I really liked in high school. As a good Catholic girl she did not want to deter me from the priesthood. And her mother thought I was a saint already. "Pinky" said at least one rosary a day for me, and we were fast friends to her dying day. At her funeral I mentioned her prayers for me and I said to her large family, "Who's going to take up the slack?"

Anyway, the call from God was clearer, and I entered the Franciscan novitiate to begin seven years of monastic rigor. I don't think the regimen had changed in five hundred years; it was . . . un-American. You had to have a sense of humor. We had a lot of laughs over simple things; we needed them. One diversion was an old German priest/teacher who was prone to mixing German metaphors into English. Hearing a disturbance in the class while writing on the board he would declare: "Stop laughing at my behind." One time he direly warned us: "Beware of girls of the opposite sex." In the year-long novitiate we didn't even see girls except on our weekly group walk. I know how prisoners feel.

friar Claude

* * *

A Gentle Hand

I had never seen a Franciscan before. The Jesuits were the models held up by the sisters who taught me in grammar school. I took the entrance exam for the well-known Jesuit high school in Boston. Things went well enough for me as I moved about the corridors of their school on the day the exam was given. I was thirteen years old and I figured I'd probably attend that school. The Russians had just launched Sputnik and I was ready to prepare myself for a career as a space scientist, to help America put a man on the moon.

The sister had told us, however, that we should take the entrance exams for three schools, so I signed up for two more. The mood in the second school was tense on exam day. The brothers looked stern and strict. About two aisles over from me another kid was buckling down to the task at hand. He was fidgeting about in nervousness when the brother in charge swooped down, accused him of cheating, gave him a "zero" on the test, and dismissed him. I trembled in fear, kept glued to my paper and left vowing not to attend that school.

FEAR AND TERROR

School number three, Columbus High School, was staffed by Franciscans. The brown robe, white cord, hood, and sandals drew my attention on exam day. The friar proctoring the exam seemed kind and said a prayer that we would do well on the test. As we began the test, however, I was struck with fear and horror. Two aisles over a kid was fidgeting. The friar came down from the desk. I'm sure that the scene from the previous school was going to repeat itself. It didn't. Instead, the friar put his hand on the boy's shoulder, invited him to relax and say a prayer.

I returned home on that Saturday morning and told my parents that I wanted to go to that school. I had no thoughts then of becoming a priest or religious, let alone one of these brown-robed friars that I had never met before. By the end of my junior year however, I had applied to the Franciscan seminary and began my journey with the friars in my freshman year of college.

Surely the hand of God was gently calling me to him on that Saturday morning in March in a classroom full of nervous eighth graders who were pondering their future. Throughout my life I have found that God's call has usually come not in the thunderbolts, but in the gentle breezes.

friar John A

* * *

Christmas in Goias

The year I was ordained a priest I went to our missions in Brazil. I finished the language course shortly before Christmas. The

superior of the mission asked me to go help out one of the
diocesan priests who was sick and had no one to assist him with
the Christmas Masses.

I went to a small rural town where I met the pastor, an elderly
monsignor who had been in the parish for many years and who
ruled it like a benign despot, even from his deathbed. He would
take care of the Christmas Masses in the town. I was to say
Masses in three rural chapels each separated from the other by
hours of travel.

SOAKED AND COVERED IN MUD

One of the parishioners had generously given up his Christmas
with his own family to take me in his truck to the chapels.
Since December is the beginning of the rainy season in Brazil,
Christmas eve was a day of persistent heavy rain. We drove for
hours over rutted roads up to the hubcaps in mud, fording
puddles that were more like small ponds, with water up to the
doors. We arrived at a small village at dusk, with darkness now
adding to the dreariness of the unrelenting rain. There was no
electricity in the town, so no festive Christmas lights. Christmas
Mass was to be at midnight, but people were already arriving
by horseback, from all the ranches in the area. They were soaked
and covered with mud.

The chapel where we were to have Mass seated about a
hundred persons. It had a small room in the back where the priest
could sleep. My Portuguese was halting, so my conversation at
the evening meal was very basic: I said a lot of "Merry Christ-
mases." The chapel had a cement floor, a very basic wooden
altar, and a few backless benches. But, with great love and
devotion, someone had set up a crèche, gaudily colored plastic
figures, placed among crepe paper flowers and holy pictures.

A Christmas homily is always a challenge! My limited vocabu-
lary made it even more so. I needn't have worried. When I
stepped out of the priest's bedroom into the chapel to begin the
Midnight Mass, I saw well over one hundred persons packed
into that candlelit little chapel. They were poorly dressed, wet
and muddy, but they were entranced by the Christmas crèche.
They sang the traditional carols as if a symphony had accompanied them.

COVERED WITH DIAMONDS

While I read my homily in my lame Portuguese, they continued to come forward to kneel before the crèche to reverence the Holy Family. It could have been covered with diamonds and their awe would not have been greater. My words were unnecessary. One young mother was an especially touching sight. She was carrying her first born, and was showing her the God who became a little baby just like her to show how much he loved her. They had walked for miles through rain and mud and darkness to see a newborn infant, to sing, to pray, to celebrate.

After Mass I went to the little room behind the chapel. My bed was a straw mattress on the floor. The light was a flickering candle. I had saved all my Christmas cards and letters from home unopened, so I could open them on Christmas night. As I lay reading them in the shadowy room, with rain beating on the tiles above my head, I was not only connected to my family and past friends. All those simple country people whom I had never seen before and would never see again had shown me where God was that night, that home was not really far away, and that I really never was a stranger. They had taken me in and welcomed me, and brought me once again home to my God in the manger! *Feliz Natal!*

friar Charley

* * *

Laughter, Peanut Butter, and "They"

The ingredients of a Franciscan vocation: laughter, peanut butter and jelly on homemade bread, seminarians' spring-time baseball—but mainly laughter—and song too around the piano at my boyhood home of 4409 32nd Street in Mt. Rainier, Maryland, on the very border of Washington, D.C.

"THEY" MIGHT BE THERE

Imagine a twelve-year-old boy in 1949 (that's me) waiting restlessly for the dismissal from Sr. Madeleine Cecelia's seventh-grade class, running to the bike rack, and pedaling home as fast as he could—down 34th Street, past Mrs. Chapman's and the fire house, an oblique left onto Rainier Avenue and then the same angle but to the right onto 32nd Street—across Upshur and Varnum to Webster and 32nd (my corner). While pedaling, the hopes become more vibrant—that "they" might be there. "They" were the Franciscan seminarians: Evan, Venard, Demetrius, Canisius, Owen, John, Sylvester, Norbert, Kenan, Dominic, Conrad, Lucian, Myles, Cajetan, Stephen, Francis, Bede, Boniface, Neil, John Forest, Regis, Cassian, Jordan, Ronald, Matthew (who later preached eloquently at my first Mass), and my cousin Alexander, better known to the whole world as "Dagwood."

"They" would come on a free afternoon—not all at the same time or the same day, of course. My mother ("Aunt Vera" to the bunch) could not have possibly fed twenty-six husky young men with voracious appetites all at one time (though I think I hear her saying from heaven, "Oh yes I could have").

MIRTH AND LAUGHTER

Four or five would come at a time, and as I would enter the driveway, I could already hear the mirth and laughter. It was off the bike, down with the kick-stand, and up the stairs in a bound—all in one sweeping microsecond. Then I would be immersed in their Franciscan joy until "they" began their mile trek back to the seminary, Holy Name College, for prayer and study.

Some Saturdays I would go and watch them play baseball. Steve had a magnetic glove at third base, Conrad was a new Phil Rizzuto at short, and Dominic had precision control on the mound. After "they" won (most of the time), we would head for "collation"—homemade bread with towering gobs of peanut butter and jelly—and more laughter.

Ordination for them and high school for me. Shortly they were in Brazil and Japan and Bolivia and New York—while I struggled with the fourth declension in Latin and the laws of energy in physics. Then in my senior year there was the question: What am I to do with my life? Marriage? Priesthood? Religious life?

A PERMANENT DEPOSIT

The young friars' laughter was becoming more and more an echo, though permanently deposited in my memory bank (it still is at age 58). My high school mentors were the Augustinian friars. Their dedication and hard work and care for me and my classmates were inspiring (again still so at age 58). We were the pioneer class, the first graduating class of Archbishop Carroll High School in Washington, D.C., and they wanted to make sure we got the school off to a good start. They did. Today in different times with different needs the school still flourished— a model of evangelization to the African-American teenage boys and girls of Washington, D.C.

Then there was "Father Hughes"—the best possible model of the diocesan parish priest—prayerful, present, and resilient. Everything about him was priestly (still I remember at age 58). And, of course, there were the young ladies of my life, lovely candidates for the sacrament of marriage—attractive, caring, and pretty.

So what was I to do with my life? I talked to my mom and dad, my brothers Robert and Jim, my friends Dave and George— and to God—and decided to cast in my lot with the laughter, peanut butter, and "them."

In short order, to be sure, I found out there was much more. There was the discipline and hard work, the awareness that in the land of laughter and peanut butter all was not peaches and cream (still so at age 58). The Lord is good. He gives us a taste of resurrection before he asks us to take up his cross and follow him—and often along the way he renews our hopes and dreams with the energy of the Holy Spirit.

Life as a priest in the Franciscan brotherhood has been and is a good way to live out a brief human existence—gradually by the grace of God coming to know with the heart the meaning of the birth, death, and resurrection of Jesus of Nazareth in the spirit of St. Francis of Assisi—for myself and the scores of good people that God has sent into my life.

Half of the original "they" of 1949 at 4409 32nd Street are now with the Lord or chose another path along the way. The other half are still in Brazil, Japan, Bolivia, and New York— forty-seven years later! God bless them all wherever they may be.

Thank God for the laughter and peanut butter—but "they" were the hook of my Franciscan vocation.

friar Edward

Surprised by Humility

When I asked my father if I could go to the high school seminary to study to become a Franciscan priest, I was looking at thirteen years of testing and preparation ahead of me. It was to be a long haul. Dad, John Cronin, in his wisdom said: "Kev, it's your life, if this is what you want, you have my permission. But don't ever forget that if you change your mind, the door is always open."

Off I went to Callicoon, New York, a fourteen-year-old idealist who had gone to Mass and Holy Communion at Our Lady of the Snows Church by bike, every day on my own since I first received the Lord in the second grade at St. Anne's Church, Garden City, Long Island. And everything was still in Latin.

STRANGE WORD

When in the seminary we often heard about the strange word *humility*. That along with obedience seemed to be favorite words for those times in the church. I never seemed to understand though what this humility was all about. Even though a certain prefect of discipline seemed to do everything in his power to bring about that desired effect in each of us, often saying words like: "We don't need you here!" "Straighten up or you'll find yourself on the train to go back to wherever you came from."

New seminaries were being built, and they all seemed full. There didn't seem to be any shortage of vocations in those early sixties. So, you had to work hard and prove yourself to get through! Sixty-five young idealists began their preparation with me in 1962. After thirteen years of hard work, testing by the friars as well as the changing church and culture we were living in, only seven of those "originals," as we used to call ourselves, were finally ordained. After being a priest for twenty-one years now, I am the only one left of those originals who began our journey for Franciscan priesthood together in 1962. As a matter of fact I am the *last* person still in our Order to go through St. Joseph Seraphic Seminary in Callicoon for four years of high school and two years of college. Little bit of historical trivia to prepare you for Jeopardy! The college section was closed after our class, so was our novitiate in Lafayette, New Jersey! Was this our lesson in humility . . . to close places?

AM I NEXT?

After two years of struggling with the Vietnam War and with our own identity at the Catholic University of America, where we all majored in philosophy, many young friars left the habit and sandals behind. It was always so sad to see guys you loved, who had truly become brothers, go their separate ways. Always a test. "Will I be next?" "Why do I stay?" Even priests who had taught us left. Well, I hate to say it but after all those years, and three more years of theology, it only seemed natural to feel that I "deserved to be ordained"! I had worked hard. I made it through the rain and the pain. I made it through all the game-playing! Almost like "God, you owe me now!" Anyone working for such a long-range goal lasting thirteen years must have feelings like this. It's only normal.

Before ordination I decided to go to confession in our famous church in New York City, St. Francis of Assisi on thirty-first Street, near Penn Station. I went "into the box" to a friar I knew and respected, Fr. John Felice. I told him I thought I'd be ready for priesthood, but I shared with him a few ambiguities about myself and my mystery which didn't yet quite seem ready even after all those years. Normal sexual issues for a twenty-five-year-old man trying to be celibate. I'll never forget what John told me: "When that bishop puts his hands on your head, Kevin, he is choosing you for God, and God will use you just the way you are." I have never forgotten those good words of Good News.

FINALLY UNDERSTOOD

Well, when Cardinal Bernardin put his hands on my head, on that wonderful feast of the Exaltation of the Cross, September 14, 1974, I felt the meaning of those words, and I finally understood humility. As a matter of fact, I was surprised by humility. I who had come to this moment and this event that I thought I was so deserving of, could do nothing but fill up with tears of gratitude at the great gift that God was bestowing on me. I asked God: "Do you really know what you are doing, ordaining me?" I finally realized that this calling was "not my own doing, but purely God's gift" (Ephesians 2:81). I began to understand the mystery of God's plan, who chooses the merest children, the lowly, to do his work. I, all of a sudden, was filled not with my own self-righteousness, but with the deepest gratitude for God's gracious gift of the outpouring of the Holy Spirit, bestowed on me through the laying on of hands. This was one of those profound moments of realization of the ultimate sublime mystery at the deepest levels of my being, where I was encountering God's action and movement in my life at my very core. The other reality was knowing that what I was receiving as "pure gift," not earned reward, must be as freely "given as a gift" (Matthew 10:8).

CRY LIKE A BABY

As every other priest present laid his hands on my bowed head sharing the power of the priesthood, the power of the Church, the power of the Holy Spirit, I could do nothing but cry like a baby, with tears of gratitude of how God has used each of these men and will continue to do so, and now would begin to use me. That day and many times since I've been a priest God has given me that wonderful gift of being "surprised by humility." It wasn't something I could teach myself, it would only be something God alone could reveal . . . when I was ready. Someone once said: "When the student is ready, the teacher will come." I was never more ready. To God alone be all honor and glory now and forever and ever. Amen.

friar Kevin

* * *

One Red Rose

God uses more the little things, the little people, the small moments of this world to motivate and change. When I was nearing the end of my fourth year of college and I had this urge (others might name it a "call") to become a priest, but was completely unsure whether I should entertain and act on the thought, I came across somewhere a novena to St. Thérèse of Lisieux, the Little Flower. She was somehow associated with roses, I learned. So during the novena I prayed that God would show me by the sign of one red rose that I should apply to the Franciscans.

On the last day of the novena, and still no rose of any color, I was walking to a job that I had in an auto parts store when I saw in the window of a house a large bouquet of roses. Pink roses. But stuck in the midst of them was one red rose. "That's it," I said to myself. And it was it. I applied, was accepted, and have been a Franciscan friar now for forty-five years.

Was it a divine sign, a grace, a simple accident? I don't know. But such a small thing helped to shape my life. I prefer to think that it is in such small ways that God shapes us and directs us.

friar Roderic

* * *

Beyond the Mountain

The fact that I am a Franciscan today is the greatest proof in my personal life of the existence of the Holy Spirit. The Spirit indeed loves to work with unsuspecting souls: I never had known a Franciscan, I never had seen a Franciscan house, I knew nothing about them until I wrote their vocation director and asked for an interview.

OUT THERE

Anyone who grew up in the country will understand my worldview as a child. Living in the foothills of the White Mountains in New Hampshire, I was reared with the idea that all that was exciting in the world was "out there," not in my quiet hometown of Ashland. We were bystanders watching a distant world. I knew that, whatever I was destined to do, wherever my personal adventure would take me, my future was out there, beyond the mountain.

I didn't realize as I was growing up that the most important parts of my life were being formed and nurtured. My parents worked and sacrificed so that my brother and I could have a good education and a better life. My family taught me the meaning of love and commitment.

WHITE CLAPBOARD CHURCH

Together with them, our gentle parish priest and the beautiful simple people who worshiped week in and week out in our tiny white clapboard church, showed me the meaning of faith. These gave me roots: family, love, faith, and commitment.

But then came the time to fly. I saw my first football game at age fourteen. The adventure was beginning! Later, I entered Boston College, where I had my first pizza at age 18! This was living! It was during those years of college—learning, making new friends, trying to understand the world—that I grew to appreciate the blessings that God had given me—blessings that I had taken for granted as a child. A desire to respond to these gifts, plus the tremendous emphasis on social problems and volunteerism in the 1960s, led me to join the Boston College lay apostle program after graduating.

PAYBACK

I became a volunteer with the idea that I would serve for one year to sort of "pay back" God for all he had given me, and then I would rush back to the States and get on with my real life—get a job, a red sports car, a state-of-the-art stereo system, and a modern house in the suburbs . . . pursuing the great American dream. The next three years changed my life.

MOST IMPORTANT LESSON

As a lay volunteer, I was sent to the island of Jamaica. Upon arriving, I was driven to the ends of the earth, handed a stack of books and told that I was to teach more than a hundred Jamaican students. The goal was to enable them to take the formidable Cambridge Exams, which would determine their entire future. I learned responsibility, dedication, and the meaning of adventure in short order. But the most important lesson I learned is still part of my daily life, and that is this: you learn what you are called to be from the people you are called to serve. I still live by that.

An example of that lesson has stayed with me through the years. One evening, I accompanied the school nurse to bring leftover food to an old man whose wife had died and who now lived alone. After walking hill and gully for an hour we arrived at his clearing only to hear a weak groaning coming from an incredibly poor small bamboo hut with a dirt floor. We ran to the opening which served as a door expecting to find Mr. Edwards sick and probably dying. He was in the center of the hut in a kneeling position next to the only object in the hut, a mat for sleeping. That was all; there was absolutely nothing else in there. When he heard us he turned toward us. His smile made his face break into a million wrinkles and as his eyes danced he said, "Welcome!" We rushed to him, "Mr. Edwards, is there anything wrong? Are you hurt?" As we helped him to his feet he said, "Oh, no. I was just praying . . . thanking God for all the blessings that he has given me!"

THANKING!

He said *thanking!* This man had nothing and no one in the world, and he was *thanking* God. I stepped back and could almost feel the American dream fall in pieces to the bottom of my mind. What faith! He is so rich! I am so poor!

During those years in Jamaica my priorities changed. My values were turned upside down. I began to think of things . . . eternal things that would last forever. That is when the Holy Spirit made a most interesting play. In the jungle, twenty miles from civilization, I ran across—just happened to find—a book lying around. The book was called *Guidepost*. It contained pictures and short descriptions of every religious order in America. How the book got there, why I picked it up, I'll never know. I wrote to three groups based on very flimsy hunches. One never wrote back, another was anxious to fly down to interview me, and the third, the Franciscans, gently offered to meet with me when I returned home that summer.

I liked the last approach and I accepted it. I only knew that Franciscans were supposed to be simple and joyful. I understood them to be close to the earth and approachable. There was something inside me that urged me to throw my lot in with the friars and let God take care of the details. And so I entered the Franciscans.

When I look back at this uncharacteristic way for me to make an important decision, when I realize the almost casual reasons that swayed me, I know now how much the Holy Spirit was active during that time of decision-making. I can attribute it to nothing else.

I entered the Franciscans at an exciting and painful time in the Church, right after Vatican II. The Church was having a nervous breakdown. I knew a little of the old and I was part of forging the new. There were many more questions than answers during those days. Thank God, we were able to weather the storms because of solid formation directors and understanding mentors.

My first full-time ministry was at St. Joseph's parish in East Rutherford, New Jersey. There the people taught me what it meant to be pastoral. They helped me realize that all parishes are full of good people and untapped potential waiting to be unleashed. It is our duty to encourage them and let that energy form the faith community. Working in youth ministry, I was inspired by the goodness of teenagers and young adults. They truly want to live worthwhile lives. They look to the friars for guidance.

WHAT'S SO SPECIAL?

I was then asked by the Province to go into vocation work. Again a familiar pattern developed. Just as it was the people in Jamaica who helped me find my vocation, working with young men looking into the friars changed my values as a friar and profoundly affected my future. I interviewed and talked to hundreds of men who asked what a Franciscan was, what do Franciscans do, why do men become friars, and the like.

Repeatedly being asked, leads you to ask questions of yourself. I had to look at my life as a friar. The men I interviewed were really asking me what was different or special about being a friar. I had to offer them something that they didn't already have. I had to offer a different way to live, a different way to witness.

AT IT AGAIN

At the same time we friars were being asked by our Franciscan leaders and were being directed by Franciscan documents to return to the spirit of our founder, to live simply and have a preferential option for the poor. The documents asked us to live *among* the poor as well as work *with* them. Thus I was being asked to take this direction from above and below—from our Franciscan leaders and from the young men who came looking for a radical way to live the Franciscan life. The Holy Spirit was at it again, this time not so subtly.

Upon leaving the vocation office I joined the Maverick Street community in East Boston. This was a group of Friars who had formed an "inserted community" in a poor section of Boston across the street from public housing projects. Their community, based on recent documents, was founded not so much for a specific work as for a Franciscan presence. We lived and prayed together, but we all did different work. One friar taught school, one was a counselor for alcoholics, one ran a thrift store, and one worked in a shelter. I was asked to help out in the local parish desperately short of staff.

My experience with this community was enriching and joy-filled. It was truly a family. Besides attending to the needs of the people, many "unchurched" but close to the Lord, we were able to start a food pantry and a much-needed *family* shelter. I became more settled with my life as a friar, ministering and living in a manner that was consistent with what I was shown by those I served and by the Order's directives.

ALL RIGHT HERE

Now I am continuing on that road, but in a different city. I work at St. Francis Inn in Philadelphia. It is a soup kitchen in the heart of Kensington, one of the most desperate neighborhoods in America—a neighborhood filled with the homeless, drug addicts, prostitutes, people with mental problems and destitute families. All the excitement, activity, and adventure I could ever hope to have is all right here. I often smile and wonder what my father, having worked so hard to give me a better life, would think if he knew I would wind up in a ghetto.

UNRELENTING LESSONS

But I am rich beyond measure, because the Spirit continues to teach me this unrelenting lesson: I am taught what I am called to be by the people I am called to serve. Daily I am transformed.

The lonely bag lady who left me three pennies under her plate of soup as a tip, is the widow in the temple giving from her want: I am taught generosity. A disabled veteran limps in each night on crutches, high on drugs to which he became addicted after his mind and body were damaged in Vietnam: I am taught the value of peace. The prostitute in her eighth month of pregnancy who came in recently so exhausted she fell asleep on the floor, woke up and asked us to call her family in Delaware (they dropped everything and came to get her), is the prodigal daughter. I am taught repentance. A woman pushes a cart all day collecting cans who, in responding to my "Thank God it's not raining," told me rain or not she thanks God every day, because she has been given one more chance: I am taught gratitude. An eighty-year-old woman who daily picks through the trash that we put out in front of our thrift store smiled and told a young college volunteer that she hopes the young girl's life will be as happy as hers has been: I am taught where true joy lies.

AT THE MASTER'S FEET

So now I know what lies beyond the mountain; it is a vastly different expression of the same, gentle Spirit that was with me in my sheltered hometown. Growing up, I felt the Spirit breathe and move in the life of my family and in those who prayed in that small white church. And now that same Spirit, looking very, very different, but no less alive, is moving in the hearts of the homeless, the prostitutes, the addicts, the mentally disturbed, and all those who have fallen from society's grace. And they teach me . . . teach me what I am called to be. And I sit respectfully at their feet.

friar Michael

2

My Greatest Pleasure

How excellent are your faithful people, O Lord!
My greatest pleasure is to be with them.
Psalm 16:3

Filene's Basement

Forty years of Franciscan priestly ministry have passed so quickly. I keep demanding a recount, but that mystical biblical number of forty always comes out the same. During the first of those forty years I lived at St. Anthony Shrine, deep in the heart of Boston's downtown shopping district. An elderly woman stopped me one day and told me how much she envied my life. Newly ordained and naive, I assumed that she was impressed by the spirit, the life and the joy of St. Francis whom we friars were attempting to follow.

But when I asked her why she envied my life she replied, "Because you live right across the street from Filene's Basement, and can run right over there any time you want." Her answer still convinces me of a basic fact of life—location, location, location. Just "being there," in a particular place, has always seemed very important to me. "Don't do something, just stand there."

friar Brennan

* * *

Why Do You Come?

I'll start off piously (wait till you read further); that's what is expected of priests in prose. The longest journey is from the head to the heart. I want to tell you about one such journey.

Her name was Elsie. In a new assignment, I was visiting a chronic-care wing in a large county hospital. I had the names of all our parishioners there and gave Elsie's name to the nurse. She directed me and said firmly: "Good luck." Elsie was in a wheelchair, her head bowed down. I went into my song and dance: "Hi, I'm your friendly, local, neighborhood priest and I've come to visit you." No response, she did not look up.

After a while I mumbled I would be back in two weeks. "Don't bother," she said clearly. The second time, the same reaction. As I left, she shook her head and said: "Why do you come?" On the drive back to the parish, I asked myself: "Why do I come?" Why bother? I was not wanted. But I kept thinking (praying?), God is love, love your neighbor, and "If you love only those who love you, what credit is that to you?" (Luke, 6:32). So I made a decision to love, for better or for worse, in good times and in bad. The next time, the routine was the same, but when she grumbled: "Why do you come?," I said, "Because I love you, Elsie." She looked up for the first time and stared. "See you soon," I said, and I could feel two eyes on the back of my neck as I moved into the hallway. I said "I love you" in my head, but it was a start.

The next time I visited she watched me intently, sort of nodding her head at my conversational attempts. Again, my parting words, "I love you Elsie," and she allowed a smile. Each visit was more refreshing and she began to share her thoughts . . . and occasional blasphemies against God and the medical profession. The disease (multiple sclerosis, I think) was arrested at this time. Her response was healthier too, towards me and others and towards God. We got along famously, and her rejoinder to my regular greeting was a fervent: "I love you too!" Often we held hands as we talked. One time she came up with some pictures of a beautiful mountain village in Switzerland where she spent some of her childhood. And I shared with her stories of my childhood in beautiful, downtown Passaic, New Jersey.

My term in the parish was ending, and I told Elsie I would be leaving soon for another assignment. She was up in years, and the disease activated again. She was failing each time I saw her, and she became bedridden. Within a week or so of my transfer, she died.

friar Claude

Dewey Said No

Any of us can single out people who have been teachers for us in learning how to live. Perhaps the teaching extended over many years, as with my parents, or perhaps just one incident made us a better person. Dewey Romagnoli was a senior in high school when I was a freshman. The oldest son, he had to take on the responsibilities of adulthood when his father died, helping his mother to keep the family together. But he also had time for the school sports and was captain of the basketball team: a good player and the leader of the others. We all admired Dewey, looked up to him.

On Friday evenings there would be a dance in the school gym. When the team played at home there would be a half-hour or so to dance after the game. This particular evening I was standing outside the locker room when Dewey came out and stood talking to a friend of his, also an athlete, but in football. His friend, Carmen, suggested that Dewey join a few other guys at a party and have a drink. Dewey refused. "Come on," urged Carmen, "a little bit won't hurt you." "No," insisted Dewey. "not during basketball season." That simple act by Dewey, whom I respected, adhering to a principle, had a great influence in my life. The examples that we provide for each other, often unintentionally, are necessary.

friar Roderic

* * *

The Reunion

For twelve years, from 1958 to 1970, I was a faculty member at our Franciscan Junior Seminary, St. Joseph's, in a beautiful country town named Callicoon. The lasting value of those years, as I recall them now, consists in having been part of something much greater than myself. The daily routine had its bright moments and its dull ones, but for the most part it was what the liturgical year calls "ordinary time." In retrospect the seminary experience has given me a deeper appreciation of Jesus' parable of the mustard seed, with its slow and imperceptible growth.

TOP COP

In June 1991, the graduation class of 1966 held a silver anniversary reunion at Siena College. Fr. Bill McConville, a member of the class and president of Siena, hosted the weekend gathering. Eighteen alumni attended, many accompanied by their wives. At last these women who had patiently endured repetitious tales of seminary life could put faces on the names of friars who had tormented their husband during their adolescent years. Of the class, only three were still friars. I thoroughly enjoyed hearing the jubilarians reminisce. Now they were in their early or mid-forties, eight to ten years older than I had been when I was their English, Latin, and physical education teacher, their baseball and hockey coach. But above all, I had been their "prefect of discipline." What an awesome title! What a horrible job! It was my task to be top cop, drill sergeant, and enforcer of law, order, and civilized behavior. All of this was supposed to be done with a dash of motherly heart and fatherly concern.

Twenty-five years earlier, Dennis had been a special thorn in my sandal. His wife said, "Dennis, Fr. Brennan doesn't seem at all like the ogre you described to me." So I smiled at Dennis and replied, "Well, you know Marie, some people have the gift of bringing out the worst in others."

LIKE DOGS

David's recollection made me feel pretty good. "You treated us all the same. You were very fair and played no favorites." Then I wondered if he meant what Jerry Kramer of the Green Bay Packers said about his coach. "Mr. Lombardi was very fair. He treated all of us in the same way—like dogs."

I asked Jim if he would like to change in any way a comment he had made many years before. He had just finished a grueling phys. ed. hike to the top of the highest neighboring hill. I had been pushing him and all his classmates to run the entire distance. He was fifteen years old, and I was thirty. In an exhausted voice he said to his friend, "Well, if an old man like Fr. Brennan could do it, I guess we ought to be able to do it." *Old* is a relative term.

One alumnus said that the seminary years had been the happiest ones of his life. This made me think that the past twenty-five years had really been hard for him. But I accepted his words as a compliment, in the spirit in which they had been spoken.

UNANIMOUS

What made me feel so happy was the unanimous expression of gratitude the alumni expressed for what they had received, not just in education, but in spiritual formation and appreciation of life's real values. I remembered all the friars and lay people on the staff who had created the atmosphere that had formed these men. I was just one of the friars who had been there for many years. Even though we have been scattered in many different directions, there still exists an extraordinary bond among us.

JUST THERE

At the final reunion dinner the graduates continued to recount hilarious memories of the friars and their eccentricities, memories which may not have seemed so funny at the time of the actual happening. It was evident that it was *who* the friars were, not so much what they did, that was of influential and lasting value. We were "just there" every day, doing the countless small tasks that make up daily life. Now it was rewarding to see eighteen mustard seeds, fully grown, and to know that along with many others, I had a role and a part in their growth.

Today the seminary is closed, the buildings and campus are a government job corps training school. Young people who need educational and vocational guidance are being provided with both, so the mustard seeds are still flourishing.

PILGRIMS AND STRANGERS

The demise of St. Joseph's is a powerful reminder that we are pilgrims and strangers in this world, as St. Francis believed. Real estate is not our business or concern. As great as the seminary was in its day, it has passed on. Even greatness is transitory. But, I am still here. Go figure! You never know.

friar Brennan

* * *

A Funny Thing Happened

It was often difficult getting teachers of religion for the teenagers in the first parish I was in. One person said to me: "I would have difficulty with their deep theological questions." I don't remember it that way at our open question-box sessions.

Couples "going steady" were the rage then. Easily, most of the questions dealt with relationships—specifically the "how far can (I) we go" variety. I remember one card, signed "junior boy" which asked: "Why can't I have an afare [sic] with my girlfriend?" Noting that, I answered, "If you can't spell it kid, you can't have it."

HE'S OUT

In the parish we had an excellent cook who was born somewhere in central Europe and spoke six languages—none of them well. She answered the phone for an hour each afternoon, which usually coincided with my nap. People would call and she would reply indignantly, "He's asleep!" Apprised of this I told her: "Just say he's out, that's all, he's out." Stirring a few days later, I heard this conversation: "He's out yes, yes, call back in an hour? OK, he'll be up by then."

One time I was helping her move to another room in the friary. There was a small metal container on the bureau; I picked it up and showed it to her. She held her palm over her heart an said softly, "My husband." I mentioned maybe we could build some fitting placement for the urn in the book case. "Never mind," she said, "he was a son of a bitch."

SOFT TOUCH

At the Philadelphia soup kitchen, a young woman junkie was opportuning the nuns for money. Not believing her pleading, they refused her. She went around to the other entrance where a Franciscan Brother who was a soft touch gave in and handed over a few dollars. Coming back waving the bills, she hollered to one of the Sisters: "I got the money from the Brother, f . . . you Sister!"

I guess life can be obscene and hilarious at the same time as long as there is hope for something better. Oscar Hammerstein wrote:

> I know the world is filled with troubles and many injustices. But reality is as beautiful as it is ugly. I think it is

just as important to sing about beautiful mornings as it is to talk about slums.*

Here's to beautiful mornings, especially to the one that will never end.

friar Claude

* * *

Young Ministers

In mid-November of 1995, a sophomore named David at St. Bonaventure University approached me about "something very important." He wanted to plan a surprise baby shower for one of the campus ministers, Jason, and his wife Colleen, who were expecting their first child in late December.

David had big plans. First, he wanted to sign out one of the rooms in the ministry center for the shower. He also wanted some funding so the baby shower could include certain essentials such as food, beverage, decorations, and gifts. Next, he wanted to borrow one of the campus ministry cars so that he and others could go into nearby Olean and pick up the necessary items. I was impressed by David's enthusiasm and good will, so I assured him that campus ministry would certainly support his efforts in this regard. I wondered to myself, however, if David could pull this plan off.

David began by quietly meeting with myself and about ten or twelve enthusiastic students to plan a strategy to make this shower happen. We agreed upon a date and time, and devised a scheme to get Jason and Colleen over to the ministry center at the proper time. The plan in effect was to switch over to the ministry center the regular evening prayer which Jason and Colleen usually hosted in their residence hall apartment. We reasoned that this plan could get them over there without suspicion of anything unusual going on; simply a change of scenery for prayer! We hoped it would be a complete surprise.

Students eagerly volunteered to get decorations, bring party favors, purchase gifts, bake brownies, buy snacks and soda, and

---

*Quoted in *The Best of Bits and Pieces*, Fairfield, N.J.: Economics Press, 1994, ed. Arthur F. Lenehan.

send out invitations. David offered to plan a prayer service and to do some baking. My role was easy. I sat there very impressed!

IN THE BURGANDY ROOM

Over the next several days, the students went to work on their agreed upon responsibilities. There was a hushed enthusiasm around the ministry center in the days leading up to the shower. Finally the big day arrived. Jason and Colleen opened the doors to the Burgundy Room in the ministry center shortly after ten P.M. Immediately, the hundred or so students, faculty, staff, and friars who had gathered for the event shouted "surprise"! Jason and Colleen stopped dead in their tracks. Their faces reflected the astonishment that touched them to the core. For a few moments everyone froze. The crowd watched Jason and Colleen waiting for a further reaction from them. They simply gazed at the crowd as if spellbound. Jason finally broke the ice, "Well, somebody do something!"

The crowd began welcoming and congratulating Jason and Colleen with bright smiles and warm embraces, as the atmosphere in the Burgundy Room reflected the festive decorations the students had hung. David then led the prayer service which he had prepared. Jason and Colleen knelt down together, hand in hand, during the prayer service. Tears of appreciation and joy trickled down their cheeks as they praised God in word and song. I could hear "sniffles" coming from different parts of the room as it was apparent that the prayer and the circumstances were touching the hearts of many. Following prayer, the evening continued with friendship, food, conversation, and of course gifts for the baby. What a fantastic event it was!!

THE REAL MINISTERS OF THE GOSPEL

I have commented to many people that the baby shower for Jason and Colleen was the best campus ministry program of the year. It was a genuine experience of love, faith, prayer, and friendship. And it came about entirely due to the initiative of college students who wanted to do something significant for a young married couple who had become very special to them.

POWERFULLY PRESENT

The Spirit of the Lord is like a gentle breeze. We cannot see the breeze, but we see and feel the effects of its presence as it moves branches on the trees, carries leaves in its air current, cools our bodies on a warm day, or chills us on a cold day! We cannot see the Spirit of the Lord either, but we see and feel the effects of its presence whenever anyone opens their hearts and responds in love to its promptings. I truly believe that I saw and felt the effects of the Spirit of the Lord in the planning and celebration of the baby shower for Jason and Colleen. The love of God was powerfully present in the Burgundy Room that evening. It warmed our hearts and freed our spirits. We experienced the faith community at its very best. And I realized once again that the majority of the ministers of the Gospel on a college campus are not the "professional ministers" (priests, brothers, sisters), but the young men and women walking around with book bags on their shoulders, working on their college degrees.

friar John K

* * *

The Widow's Mite

It was a cold rainy November evening. The dining room was crowded at St. Francis Inn. People anxious to get in out of the rain. Hustle and bustle, the back and forth of the overtaxed volunteers all lent to the activity of the inn. In the midst of it all came in a typical bag lady. She was very old, hunched over, wearing two or three scarfs over her head. She had on at least two coats and was carrying three shopping bags with all her earthly possessions in them. She shuffled in without a word and sat down at the table.

With all the activity and noise going on around her, she quietly ate her cheese sandwich and then sipped the soup until the bowl was dry. She gently got up, took hold of her three bags and still stooped over, left the inn and disappeared into the darkness of Kensington Avenue.

FOUR PENNIES

I waited on her table, and was anxious to set up for the waiting crowd. I quickly grabbed the bowl the old lady had used and headed toward the kitchen but then did a quick double take. I snapped my head around to look at what was under the bowl. There where she had eaten were four pennies! She had left a tip! As little as she had, she was grateful for what was given.

Would that we could all learn what real thanksgiving is from that little bag lady out there in the dark of the Philadelphia night.

friar Michael

* * *

Faith Such as This

Part of my life journey took me to Bolivia, South America. Bolivia is a land rich in heritage, alive with natural beauty, gifted with many wonderful people from different cultures, but touched by deeply rooted poverty. It was the result of oppression and injustice from both within and without its own borders.

After arriving there in June of 1981 and spending a few days to adjust to the altitude (many areas over 10,000 feet above sea level), I was taken on a tour of the friars' mission there.

We left La Paz, the capital, and headed down from the high altitude into the Yungas, a series of beautiful green valleys in the Andes Mountains. Hidden within the thick, semi-tropical, semi-jungle vegetation were many small villages populated by campesinos, subsistence farmers and largely Aymara people in this part of Bolivia. They were an ancient and proud people who lived there since before the Incas arrived in that part of South America.

Our jeep was passing along the dirt road that wound its way down from La Paz to Coroico to Caranavi when some people emerged from the trees and stopped us. I was frightened. I then spoke only rudimentary Spanish and my mind was filled with mythic images of ambushes and attacks. I soon realized that these people were friends and that we were needed in their village. Iggy (Fr. Ignatius Harding, ofm) and I left the jeep at the side of the road and climbed up a narrow path through the trees and into a small village of adobe huts with thatched roofs. Outside one of the small houses stood a young couple with a baby in their arms. The baby had died of measles. I was stunned, shocked beyond belief. I stepped back and let Iggy speak with them and the other villagers. They spoke in Spanish as well as

Aymara. I missed most of the conversation, but at the end I heard the young man, the baby's father, say in Spanish, "We are very sad. Our hearts are heavy, but we know that God loves us and that he will bless our love with new life." We left a short while later. Iggy explained after we got into the jeep that this was the second baby they had lost to an illness that would have been routinely treated in the U.S.A.

I remained silent as the jeep moved on. I was soothed by the natural beauty of the scenery in the Yungas, but at the same time I was filled with mixed emotions—anger at the injustice of what I saw, and sadness for that young couple. I was wondering what the friars and other missionaries did about such horrible tragedies. I told Iggy what was on my mind and asked what was indeed being done. Before answering though, he asked a question in return, "What did you learn from that couple, John?" I had to stop. I wasn't expecting this. Then I thought of Jesus' comment about a non–Jew who sought his help in one of the Gospel stories, "Faith such as this I have not seen in all of Israel."

Faith such as that couple had I needed too. Being a missionary wasn't about fixing their problems so much as about working together and learning from one another. These people had much to offer me and indeed I feel very enriched and blessed by the many wonderful things I learned, sometimes painfully, from the people of Bolivia.

Oh, yes, the friars and others did much to try to alleviate the sufferings and help overcome the terrible injustices inflicted on the Bolivian people. Some of the Sisters who were nurses had begun a vaccination campaign to help eliminate childhood illnesses and make less likely the tragedy that I witnessed that day. But they in turn helped open our eyes to whole dimensions of life and faith and love that we never knew before.

friar John A

* * *

Hi, My Name Is Fred

It was Sunday morning, no public Masses to celebrate, no missions to preach, a rare Sunday morning for a priest and I was going to enjoy it by heating up the coffee pot and hiding behind the Sunday papers. I had just sat down and poured the first cup of coffee when the phone rang. "Hello," said the voice, "I'd like to speak with Fr. Brennan please" (Fr. Brennan Connolly was one of the friars in my community at the time.) I told the man my name and explained that Fr. Brennan was away. I asked if I could take a message. "My name is Fred. I'm at a residence for AIDS patients. I spoke with Fr. Brennan last week. He was so kind, he really seemed to understand and listen. I thought that if he were there, he'd come over. I'm dying and I'm ready to make my peace with God. Could you come instead, Fr. John?"

Of course I said yes and went to the chapel to get the Eucharist as well as the holy oil for the Anointing of the Sick. This was an automatic response, but as I went to get my coat and car keys my fears took over. I knew that they were self-centered and irrational fears, but nevertheless they were there.

Though well-informed about HIV and AIDS, the questions came tumbling into my mind: "Who is this Fred? Can I touch him? He has AIDS. Who are the other people in his residence? What are they like?" I felt embarrassed at having such thoughts, but I couldn't shake them.

I arrived at the home that housed Fred and several other men who were dying of AIDS. I was very warmly received, offered some coffee and pastry, and talked briefly with the other men. They quite obviously loved and cared for Fred very much. They were scared also. He was the first of them who was going to die. They asked me to pray with them. I was touched by that, and calmed. We went up to Fred's room. They introduced me to him, then left us alone.

CAN I TOUCH HIM?
Fred lying back in his bed, appearing very weak and frail spoke first. "So you're the one I spoke with." "That's me," I said, and sat down beside him. We made a bit of small talk, then he gave me his life story—"Just the short version," as he put it. When

he was finished, he smiled and said, "Well, let's go down to the reason I called you here. You'll have to help me sit up if we're going to do this right." I reached behind Fred's back and gave him a gentle push. At this point I wasn't afraid of touching him. My irrational fears had left. I had the very rational fear of harming him because he was so frail. "You'll have to do better than that," he told me, "There's no muscle left in my body. You've got to do the work." I then gave him a good push. He sat up straight and I helped position several pillows behind him. We prayed. I heard his confession, anointed him, and shared the Eucharist with him. With tears in his eyes he thanked me and I left.

After bidding farewell to the other residents I went out to my car to start on my way home. Just as I started the ignition a tremendous peace came over me. I sat in stillness and quiet for about fifteen minutes before I actually drove away. Then the realization came. I had met Jesus. He was there, in that room, in Fred.

Fred had called to ask me to serve him. In my fumbling way I honored his request. But he gave me so much more. Although I'm far from being a St. Francis, I thought of his encounter with the leper outside Assisi. That was a moment of genuine conversion for him, of embracing not only the leper, but his own deepest fears in the light of Christ's love. It was the one moment of his life that he recalled in his testament that he wrote at the end of his life.

Fred's family came to our friary chapel a week later for a memorial service. At that time I realized that Fred's story will be part of my life, part of my own testament to the wonderful workings of God's love for us.

friar John A

* * *

One of These Days, Alice!

I first met Alice Fitzpatrick when I was studying theology at the Washington Theological Union back in the early seventies, living at Holy Name College, the Franciscan formation house. Alice used to come and visit one of our friars who was a recovering alcoholic. Alice was still very actively drinking.

TOUGHEST IRISHMAN IN WASHINGTON

The friar often asked if I would take Alice home, somewhere in Georgetown. She would be inebriated and tell me "I am the toughest Irishman in Washington, D.C.!" She was actually very amusing when intoxicated, as I learned after taking this trip with her many times over the years. She had a masters in social work from Fordham University. Much like myself, a native New Yorker, I liked hearing her Bronx accent. It made me feel at home. After a while Alice would ask for me instead of our recovering friar. Maybe she thought I was easier. Maybe she enjoyed me. I don't know.

Those last years preparing for comprehensive exams were indeed challenging ones for me. If we did not pass, we couldn't get ordained. I was at the end of a thirteen-year preparation . . . talk about delayed gratification! As Alice used to say: because I went all the way through since the high school seminary in Callicoon, that "I was one of the last real vocations!" Ha! Alice used to call repeatedly, and drop over at the spur of the moment. Idealistically I used to have to "take care of Alice." She was rather clever, intelligent, and a manipulative red-haired wild Irish colleen, at least twenty years older than myself.

ENDLESS SMOKING

I remember on one of our trips she begged me after fumigating the car with her endless smoking, and intoxicated breath, that she "needed a milk shake!" So, I stopped right in the middle of Georgetown off Wisconsin Avenue to stop at a Roy Rogers to get one for her. She had to get out and get it with me. Hanging all over me, I purchased her drink. We walked out the door, she took one sip, and tossed it across the street! One of these days Alice! I could have cried my eyes out. I was helpless, nothing I could do. I dropped her off, and went to a prayer meeting at Georgetown University that night.

I told the group of over three hundred people how helpless I felt about Alice. Only God could do something. I was asking for a miracle, and "I was turning it over" as they say in AA.

LIKE A MOTHER

I saw Alice the next day, and went the extra mile in risk taking. She had a little on her breath, but not bad. She was rational. On the front steps of Holy Name, I told her that my mother died when I was a little boy, and that maybe she could be like a mother to me. Well, I couldn't believe how moved Alice was, and how seriously she took what I had said. She did stop drinking around that time. I was another half-year in D.C. She came to my ordination.

After I went to Boston on my first assignment, I would only hear from Alice from time to time. Or perhaps we'd take a trip to the "Potter's House" on Columbia Road . . . or a walk through Rock Creek Park when I was in town and we'd renew our old friendship. Once Alice wrote me and asked for a recommendation/character reference from me many years later when she was applying for a leadership position working for the homeless. She got my recommendation and got the job!

Many years later I received a sad letter from Alice, after she had told me that she had heavy-duty cancer problems. I share it with you, because I share it on our parish missions. It's wisdom, and it's about "one of these days!"

INVITATION TO COME HOME

March 26, 1991

Dear Kevin,

Here we are in Holy Week again, for which I am very grateful. Mainly, I suppose, because I am still alive, for in December I thought that I would not make it until Christmas. But also because of the opportunity to participate again in the sacred mysteries in a very conscious— a heightened—consciousness way.

You know Kevin, we all know we're going to die, but just think how great it is to get *special notice*, as it were. Not in a morbid way or a casual "you're next," but in a deep human way. It's an invitation, Kevin, to come home. (And now I'm going to cry.)

What I'm especially grateful for is the chance to get ready. I needed this time to let God love me as he would. There is no other way to express this feeling—only to let him love me.

And I'm grateful to be allowed to be in touch with people I have loved along the way, like your own dear self Kevin.

Alice let God love her! She was prepared to hear the words of the Savior: "One of these days, you will be with me in paradise" (Lk 23:43). Alice did teach me in her living and, as hard as it was, in her beautiful dying! She had indeed stopped beating herself up, and did let God love her in this life as "all of her days he would do forever."

friar Kevin

3

Better Than Life

For Your Love, O Lord, is better than life!
As with the riches of a banquet. . . .
shall my soul be satisfied.
Psalm 63: 4, 6

I Am Loved

Of course you have—we all have—"tough times."

It seems that these times can stretch into days, weeks, months, even years! We find it difficult to see light at the end of the tunnel.

My life had become scrambled; full of confusion, doubts, and loss of direction. A feeling of impending doom and paralyzing fear made me feel as though there was little hope that my life would get better. I desperately needed love—to love myself and to allow others to love me.

A long-standing relationship had just ended on a painful note. I was struggling with a low-paying job and living (existing is more like it) in a one-room apartment. I had just stopped drinking and my brain was starting to function once again. The bills were piling up and life was becoming rather stressful, to say the least.

NOWHERE FAST

God had long ago abandoned me; or so I believed. My self-esteem was at its lowest and my self-image was just as low. Life had thrown me a curve ball and I had struck out. My life was heading nowhere—fast!

One of my hurts was the feeling I had that no one gave a damn about me . . . family, relatives, friends. Where were they? I needed them—*now*—to understand, to care, to affirm, to love, to help, to rescue me!

In the midst of my turmoil and despair I received a letter from an aunt who rarely wrote to me. What a welcome surprise!

My Aunt Anna had written me a three-page letter telling me all about family members, their lives, their situations . . . this one is in college; that one is expecting a baby; this one had a tiff with his brother—you know, family stuff. At the end of this letter she signed her name and then there was a postscript: REMEMBER— YOU ARE LOVED!

Those words jumped off the page at me. It was God speaking to me through another: "Wake up! Believe! Accept the gift. Embrace yourself."

SHE SMOKED CAMELS

How I appreciated my Aunt Anna. She was a good wife and mother—a strict disciplinarian; a no-nonsense person. She wore loafers with white bobby socks and smoked Camel cigarettes. Though a sometimes gruff and tough exterior, there was a loving, warm, and caring heart beneath this façade.

I am convinced that God comes to us in our brokenness and woundedness; and that God lifts us up from the ashes of our despair through other people. God is always present with the treasure of love.

May Aunt Anna now rest in peace and enjoy God's love, which she so generously gave to others!

friar Emmet

* * *

Naming the Baby

One of the exciting aspects of having a baby is asking, "What will we name the baby?" Often it's the name of a favorite saint. A saint that holds a special place in the heart and life of the parents. A saint who is close to God and will protect and intercede for the baby. Or the name of a favorite relative in the family. A person who has shown love, acceptance, kindness, and exemplifies all the qualities of what "family" really means.

Recently an excited young woman came to us here at St. Francis Inn with the news that she was going to have a baby. And then with a smile she told us that if it was a boy she was going to name it Benedict. Not unusual you may think, until she explained why. The name of our Thrift Shop Is St. Benedict's. She was naming her baby after a Thrift Shop! Her life is so hard, so without love, so without family that the only place she experiences any kindness, any acceptance, or any love is when she visits our store. To her that was reason enough and her baby will be called *Benedict*.

friar Michael

* * *

Touched by an Angel

Thanks to CBS, many of us who do not have a busy Saturday-night social life enjoy thoroughly the powerful and moving experiences of the angelic odd couple, Monica and Tess. Through these episodes we come to understand how God uses angels to touch upon our lives.

NAIVE

Early in my studies for the priesthood, I certainly was not an angel, but like young Samuel in the Bible, I was naive about the ways of the divine. Every October there was a bus tour from New York City to our seminary in Callicoon, N.Y., to view the spectacle of the autumn foliage. Helen came not only to see the foliage but also to experience healing for her heart condition. No sooner had she stepped off the bus and heard my welcoming voice than she asked to have the relic of St. Anthony "applied."

APPLYING THE RELIC

In my years growing up and in the thirty days I had spent in the seminary, I frankly did not know what she meant by "applying" any relic. Being of a helpful nature, I asked Helen to accompany me to Fr. Cassian Kirk, our rector, who was standing nearby. My intention was to hand Helen over to his ministerial care. When I conveyed Helen's request to him, he quickly directed me to another Friar, Fr. Cassian Corcoran, to take care of the matter. Again, I asked Helen to accompany me into the main building where we would contact a friar to "apply" the relic. We headed for the intercom near the sacristy where the relics were kept.

DO IT YOURSELF

When I reached the rector designated "applier," he responded: "Oh, you don't need me. Just go into the sacristy and get the relic for the woman." Just then, the bell rang summoning all our visitors and the student body to solemn benediction of the Blessed Sacrament.

Going into the sacristy, I noticed that Helen observed the then rule that no woman was allowed into the sacristy. She stayed at the doorway. Obtaining the relic of St. Anthony, I walked toward her and began extending my right hand containing the encased relic.

SHE OPENED HER COAT

At that moment two things happened—she opened her coat, took my relic-laden hand and "applied" both to her bosom (within which was her ailing yet rapidly pulsating heart). The second thing was that over one hundred fifty people marched passed the sacristy door on their way to benediction. All they could see was Helen's back and my blushing face as I "applied" the relic while she stormed heaven for what seemed an eternity! Helen thought I was an angel and was touched by all the trouble I underwent to obtain the relic. I think I was a dumb kid who hasn't stopped smiling.

friar Daniel

* * *

Fifteen Precious Moments

All types and all ages come to our soup kitchen here at St. Francis Inn in Philadelphia. Recently one evening three little girls came for supper. They are sisters, ages about eight, nine, and eleven. Incredible as it seems, toward the end of the month when the money runs low, their mother sends them to the Inn to eat, alone, at night and here in Kensington, in the worst area of the city.

One evening they were unusually animated. "Why are you so excited tonight, girls?" I asked. "Because today is Nancy's birthday! She's twelve!" came the reply. So then I called everyone to silence. "Today is a special day, my friends. Today is Nancy's birthday. What are we going to do about it?" Immediately the whole dining room began singing "Happy Birthday." Well, Nancy put her hands up to hide her face. She was so embarrassed and happy and smiling.

It was such a bittersweet scene. There was a little girl that had to celebrate her twelfth birthday in a soup kitchen. There was no party, no presents. no cake, no ice cream. And yet . . . there was a room full of God's poor, singing to her, making her feel like the most important girl in the world . . . if only for those precious few moments.

friar Michael

* * *

Unconditional Love

This story begins during the summer of 1987 and has continued over the past nine years. I first met a dear friend named June in June (appropriately enough) of 1987. We met in the old St. Francis Hospital in Olean, New York, during a summer ministry assignment there. (Summer supervised ministry assignments are part of the training process for a friar preparing for solemn vows and ordination.) At the time, June was in her mid-sixties and was living in Portville, New York, with her brother-in-law, Glen, who had been blind for twenty years. June had lived with Glen through all of those years and provided him with much needed tender loving care. This particular day, June was visiting Glen in the hospital after he had suffered a serious stroke.

June has recalled for me many times the details of our first encounter. I find it amusing that they are clearer now in her seventy-three-year-old mind than they are in my own thirty-seven-year-old mind. She says that I walked into the hospital room and introduced myself to her saying, "Hello, I'm Brother John and I will help you in whatever way I can." June tells me that she could see God's love and peace reflected in my eyes, and that she immediately felt that everything would be all right. She believes, as I do, that God brought me into her life at a time when she strongly needed a caring and supportive presence.

June and I have been through a lot together in the nine years since we met. We maintained a close relationship during that first year, my year of internship in campus ministry at nearby St. Bonaventure University. Glen died during that year after being transferred to a nursing home. I had the privilege of preaching at his wake and walking with June through her experience of grief.

Then, I left the Olean area and returned to Silver Spring, Maryland, to finish my studies in final preparation for ordination to the priesthood. June and I stayed in touch. Surprisingly, although she is not Catholic, June made her way down to my ordination in Silver Spring. She recruited a friend to travel with her because she wasn't able to travel alone. They flew together into Washington, D.C., and took a taxi to a hotel near the church. I was deeply moved by her unwavering commitment to be there with me on that important day, and by her personal resourcefulness which enabled her to fulfill that commitment. My first assignment following ordination was a two-year stint as a pastoral assistant in Little Falls, New Jersey. June and I continued to correspond.

When I returned to work full time in campus ministry at St. Bonaventure University in 1991, June remarked to me how happy she was that I was "coming home." Five years later, and after dozens of lunches with June at our favorite lunch spot, the Beef 'n' Barrel, it was once again time for me to move on. It was difficult to share with her the news of my upcoming transfer to New Jersey to enter the friars' preaching ministry, Ministry of the Word. I shared this with June as carefully and gently as I could on the way home in the car one day.

June's thoughts about my transition echoed my own thoughts. She said that she was sad about my leaving the area, but happy about the new and exciting possibilities for ministry that I would encounter. She seemed to understand that I simply felt that it was time for me to move on to something different. Then June was silent for several minutes. I glanced toward her as I drove and could see that she was quietly crying. She had been trying to hide her emotions from me, to keep them under control until she got home where she would be alone. She hadn't succeeded. I felt my own emotions touched by the situation as well, as my eyes moistened. It struck me at the time that this friendship would always remain because it was rooted in a particularly strong love; unconditional love.

LOVE HURTS

Since then, I have reflected on this particular experience and this significant relationship a great deal. Love hurts. There is no pretending that it does not. It is painful to genuinely care for others and then to be separated from them, whatever the reason. It is painful to experience the rejection (blatant or subtle) that eventually comes our way when we decide to love others unconditionally. Not everyone welcomes our love and concern for them. They may want us to leave them alone! Nor does everyone appreciate a stance we may take out of love. We may be ridiculed or attacked for being compassionate!

Fortunately, we are not alone in this experience. Anyone who sincerely follows Jesus Christ has experienced the inevitable pain that comes from deciding to love others unconditionally. We had been forewarned about this two thousand years ago: "anyone who wishes to come after me must deny his or her very self, take up his or her cross, and follow me." Jesus himself is our model in this regard. He was tortured and killed because he refused to stop building God's kingdom of love here on earth.

Unfortunately, the sad reality of human life is that love hurts. However, love does not stink, as claimed by a popular J. Geils Band song several years back. The commitment to sincerely care for and invest in the lives of others leads not only to pain, but more importantly to richness and depth, joy and peace, purpose and fulfillment, support and love returned to us a hundred fold. It is in our special love relationships that we most clearly and concretely see and experience who God is. Love gives life meaning because love is of God and God is love.

Every once in a while we are reminded of this truth, perhaps when we least expect it. It happens while we are alone in personal prayer, or in prayer with others during the celebration of the Eucharist. It happens with family members at home, or with friends out to dinner. It happens with friars in community or with students on a college campus. And it happened for me in March 1996 while driving an automobile with a poor elderly woman named June. Praise and glory to God who is love!

friar John K

* * *

Never Outdone

My dearest mother Annette Cronin died of cancer when I was a young boy of eleven. Dad was a detective in Harlem, whom they used to call "Big Red from Harlem." I was the youngest of three children. Ronnie was eight years older, John was four years older. We all pulled together to help us keep going. Everyone was very kind to us too.

A few years later my uncle, Arthur Keating, mom's brother, a construction worker, died when fatally knocked off the Pan Am building in New York City. A few years after that, dad and Aunt Martha began to date after dancing together at my cousin's wedding, Robert and Rosemary Frey. Aunt Martha had five children—Skip, Pete, Mary Ellen, Gerard, Chris. I was the only one still living at home of the Cronin clan. Actually I was at the high school seminary in upstate New York. So, when Dad married Aunt Martha he moved from our town of North Floral Park, Queens, to their house in Westbury, Long Island. All of her children, my first cousins, still lived at home. My place in the family now became somewhere in the middle. Only Skip was older than me of the Keating clan. So it made sense to move to where most of them lived.

Dad was very good to me. He always made sure I had a car to drive when I was old enough so I could go back to the old neighborhood, when home on vacation. He also was very generous. After selling our house he divided the money up among the Cronin children. Dad put mine in the bank, so I'd have spending money, to supplement the money I made every summer when working: three summers at a plastic factory; one at a pool in East Meadow cooking hot dogs; one picking up papers, dressed in a white sailor's uniform, at the Jones Beach Marine Theater where Louis Armstrong and Guy Lombardo were performing. Satchmo was a cool dude!

THE ONLY PLACE

The only place I ever wanted to go in this world was Assisi. I wanted to walk in the footsteps of St. Francis in the *power spot* where it all began. Dad said I should go and take a trip before entering the Franciscan Order in summer of 1968. I thanked him for the idea, thought about it, and said: "I don't think so dad, when I enter the Order I'll take a vow of poverty. Maybe I should practice it now, and give up going on this trip of my dreams."

I didn't think about this till twelve years later, after I had been working in Boston for five years as a newly ordained priest. I picked up a letter left for me at the front desk of the church one day. I still have this letter which said:

> Dear Father Kevin,
>   I thought you might like to celebrate your fifth anniversary as a priest and your tenth as a friar by going to Rome and Assisi. Enclosed is a cashier's check for $1500.
> Anonymous

Needless to say, after speaking to the guardian, Fr. Joseph Sullivan, we decided that this was a gift from the Lord who will never be outdone in generosity. And that I should go! If any poor person was given a chance like this, they would go. So, I accepted humbly. Thank you gracious and wonderful God for the hundredfold in this life! You spoil me! Keep it up!

They say when you work for the Lord, the pay isn't that great! But the retirement plan is *out of this world*! I disagree, the pay is a hundred fold in this life, and life everlasting! Generous, never outdone God, I bless you.

friar Kevin

* * *

A Christmas Miracle

One year I decided that I was going to spend Christmas that year at our infirmary. I worked there the past summer and had come to love those men. I realized that their illness and living in a friary, where most of the community would be away helping at parishes or with family, would make it improbable that Christmas would be much different than any other day. So when the Christmas break arrived and everyone in my seminary class went home, I headed up to St. Bonaventure University where our infirmary occupied the first floor of the friary. There on the ground floor lived thirteen infirm friars.

NOT FOR LONG

When Christmas eve arrived the house was as quiet as could be, very few of the nearly fifty well friars were home. After supper I decided that we needed to have a Christmas party. In the community's recreation room was a large and splendidly decorated tree and a beautiful crèche, so why waste them? I thought "take everyone seventy-five feet up the corridor into the rec room." With the nurse's permission, one by one I wheeled or walked the infirm friars into the room and around the tree. After everyone was set, I offered them some Christmas "cheer," which to my surprise everyone gladly accepted as well as handfuls of Christmas cookies and candy canes. Then I began to lead them in Christmas carols.

FATHER AMBROSE ON THE MOVE

Fr. Ambrose who was in a wheelchair could not walk or speak very intelligibly, due to a stroke a few years earlier, and arthritis. I had him sitting in the circle at one side, but he kept pushing to move his chair. After returning him to his place and adjusting him in the chair several times, I finally asked if he wanted to move to the other side. He responded affirmatively. So to the other side of the group I wheeled him, and again I tried to lead the carols. But Ambrose kept pushing in that same direction. *Now* it appeared that he wanted to sit against the far wall. Adjusting him in the chair again, I offered to move him and did. His response was unintelligible but I guessed that he wanted to be moved again. "Poor Ambrose," I thought, "once a college professor, now almost totally disabled and without much of his mind." I moved him again to where he seemed to want to be, and went back to leading those carols, which was not going too well in that most of these men were far from their best singing voice and couldn't remember many of the words, but we tried . . . "Silent Night."

HE'S STILL MOVING

Once again I became distracted by Ambrose who was trying again to move his chair now close to the piano that was at the side of the room. So without asking, I moved him right beside the piano. "There, is that better?" I asked. Well, he kept moving as if he wanted to sit on the piano bench (Ambrose couldn't sit up by himself. He had to be tied into his chair and supported with pillows on either side). Frustrated, I set him on the piano bench and sat beside him to hold him up, and again I attempted to lead the caroling . . . Deck the Halls . . . . Now Ambrose was trying to turn into the piano.

I finally realized that this man with little control over his arms and stiffened fingers probably wanted to bang away at the piano and make some noise to liven things up. "It's not New Year's Eve," I said, "but if you want to hammer away for a while, I suppose it won't hurt anything." Our caroling wasn't going very well any way.

A MIRACLE?

So I turned Ambrose into the piano and opened the cover so he could play. Now standing beside him and holding his shoulder with one hand, but turned towards the others, I once again tried to lead Silent Night. Suddenly I heard someone playing the piano! Without missing a note Silent Night was playing. I turned and it was Ambrose! and all of a sudden everyone else in the room was singing along . . . in time, and on key! Was this a miracle? This mindless old disabled friar who hadn't made any sense in years was now playing the piano and was actually leading his confreres in song! I was so excited that I began to move to go and get someone else to let them see what was happening, but as I moved, down went Ambrose. So I just stood there in amazement and for a half an hour he played (with hardly playing a wrong note despite those stiffened hands), and the others sang.

It was now getting late, time to finish the drinks and goodies, and return to the rooms so the friars could be helped to bed. I explained the whole story to the night nurse who didn't seem to believe me, then I waited for one of the other friars to return home. No one arrived before it was time for me to retire, so I just went to bed.

In the morning after I'd finished helping get each of the infirm friars up and fed we had Christmas Mass together celebrated by Fr. Gervase the guardian. After Mass I related the whole story to Gervase. He paused for a moment and replied, "Oh yeah, years ago Ambrose played the piano. He used to play at all our parties and led sing-alongs, but I didn't think he could still play after a look at those stiffened hands, and he hardly moves his arms."

I realized how sickness makes us forget a person's worth and how we can come to take them for granted. The real gift on Christmas is perhaps not some new gift, but realizing again the grace, gifts, and talents in each one of us.

Fr. Ambrose never played again, because of another stroke. But I'll never ever forget the songs he played that night . . . "Joy to the World."

friar Ron

* * *

Words of Love

My mother had been in the hospital about a week for treatment of a chronic condition, atherosclerosis (hardening of the arteries) of both legs. It was a condition that had its genesis years before, when she had surgery to reduce her high blood pressure. Now the atherosclerosis had taken its toll. I was in nursing school at the time and my mother called me one evening from the hospital. She said that the doctor had visited her and told her that there was no further medical treatment for her condition. The only recourse was to amputate both of her legs. As a nursing student, I knew that this would eventually happen, but I always kept that awareness to myself. So when my mother told me what the doctor said, I was not surprised.

The day of surgery, I went home to be with my mother. It was not easy to see my mother, with what seemed to be half a body, lying in bed after the surgery. I stayed with her for a few days and then returned to school. Each night, though, I would call my mother to see how she was.

A week to the day after her surgery, I was again speaking with my mother; she was still in the hospital. Listening to her voice I knew she was not well, and actually very sick. (My brother and I had made the decision that if my mother became critically ill no extraordinary means be used to prolong her life.) As I was talking with my mother, I had the feeling that this would be the last time I would be speaking with her. Her voice was weak and did not have the same vitality it usually did. As we were closing our conversation she said to me, "Francis, I love you, I love you, I love you." Those were the last words my mother spoke to me. Later that night my mother died.

I had always known that my mother loved me, but in her dying it seemed she wanted me to know that her love for me would continue after death, that I would always be in her heart. To this day those parting words of my mother continue to speak deeply in my heart and fill me with a love and joy that only a mother's love can give.

friar Francis

* * *

Give Them Absolution

Since my mother, Margaret Sheehan, and my father Daniel were reared in Newmarket, County Cork, Ireland, I was thrilled when the opportunity came to spend a holiday away from my doctoral studies in Rome and with my Aunt Brigid and her two sons on their dairy farm outside Newmarket.

Every afternoon around four o'clock we would have our main meal. Immediately after, Brigid would take care of the kitchen while the boys went to milk the cows. Hoping that I would be able to return to America to boast to my mother that I too was a dairy farmer for a time, I offered to assist the boys. Ah, the boys assured me that my offer was not "udder nonsense" but, nevertheless, they judged it best for the cows and for me not to let the Yank yank! So, every afternoon I took a walk around the beautiful countryside of northwest Cork.

Disappointed I set out the first day for a long walk. Little did I realize how friendly and intensely curious were all the people I met to talk to this American, and when they discovered that I was the son of Maggie Sheehan, they could not wait for me to come by in the afternoon. They had some wonderful things to relate about my mother as a young girl. It seems she was not only a good scholar, brilliant (some would say), but she was the most unselfish lovely little colleen in all of Ireland! One incident alone would convince anyone of her extraordinary kindness.

NO DECENT DRESS

As her First Communion day approached, my mother learned that Annie Griffin, her classmate, did not have a decent enough white dress to wear. Didn't my mother, little Maggie Sheehan, give her own beautiful communion dress to Annie and herself wear her cousin's white dress from the year before! Every day someone told me a new and equally remarkable act of kindness. With diligent care I made notes of all the outstanding stories and memorable feats of young Maggie Sheehan. When I returned to Rome, I could not wait to type a more permanent record of my notes as well as a more easily readable one. In a matter of hours I was able to mail the finished product to my mother in the United States. By return mail my humble almost legendary mother simply wrote three words to her gullible Franciscan priest son—Give them absolution!

The Irish are great storytellers and who can find fault with imaginative people who can't help themselves when called upon to entertain an American in need of company. Up Cork!

friar Daniel

* * *

I Didn't Know Him

I continued in the realization that I was pledged to the Lord; but I have to say for a number of years I only knew about Jesus, but I didn't know him in a personal way. That can be wearying and disappointing because the Lord in that context is on a pedestal, abstract and spiritual. He is the Word only and not the Word made flesh. In time I came to know Jesus in a personal way through prayer, especially with a young adult prayer group (Christian Family Community, Washington, D.C., 1971).

JUST IN TIME

Their directness and enthusiasm in worshiping brought God down off the pedestal. This development happened just in time because it followed on a general but real crisis with my vow of celibacy. It was discouraging to see friends and a few classmates leaving the priesthood in the early nineteen seventies. I found myself keeping my options open, so my distractions (plural) increased but never settled on one individual, and I did not become involved with anyone. In the background there was always a call to recommitment. With a lot of prayer and reflection and some very soul-stirring experiences which gave me direction, my vocation and commitment were strengthened.

VIRTUE OR SENILITY

I'm not distracted as much anymore; I can sit on a beach now and read a magazine all the way through. Although I don't know whether that's an advance in virtue or senility. I'm struck by the diverse directions in my life. I can see age slowing down my life, but spiritually the growth can go on. There is the added benefit of experience which gives confidence in my relationship to God, to others, and to myself.

Looking ahead I see eternal life as a less abstract and spiritual phrase. While I was stationed in Boston, I attended a "near-death" support group which a psychiatrist convened because the close relatives and friends of these near-death people did not give them much support. Besides myself (the theologian?), a psychologist and a philosopher were invited.

These experiences were similar to accounts of the best-selling "Life Beyond Life" (Raymond Moody, Ca. 1970) and the more recent "Embraced by the Light" and "Saved by the Light." It was a varied group and they were quite convincing. We observers were expected to ask questions.

I was interested in how these near-death experiences changed their lives. I think I would have been suspicious if they had indicated that their lives and attitudes were basically the same as before their experience. That was not the case. They said that after their experience, there was less emphasis on material things in their lives and a corresponding increase in spiritual sensitivity. Also, there was much less fear of death.

GOD: SUBSTITUTE FOR LOVE

We all yearn for a greater love, and for me this hope takes on a particular poignancy. The book *A Grief Observed* (and the movie *Shadowlands*) celebrates the late love of C. S. Lewis, the

Oxford don and writer. Late in his life a wonderful woman came into his bachelor life. But even with an idyllic relationship, Lewis writes:

> If God were a substitute for love we ought to have lost all interest in Him. Who'd bother about substitutes when he had the real thing. But that isn't what happens. We both knew we wanted something besides one another— quite a different kind of want.

THE MORE WE HAVE

If we are honest, we should admit that though our experience of human love is partially fulfilling, it also creates a longing for complete love. The more we have, the more we want. This is true of love more than anything else. St. Augustine summed it up: "You have made us for yourself, O Lord, and our hearts are restless until they rest in you."

friar Claude

4

Pure Joy

The Apostles for their part left the Sanhedrin
with pure joy, knowing they had been judged
worthy of ill treatment for the sake of the Name.
Acts of the Apostles 5:41

Three Little Chiclets

It was a bitter cold night. The thermometer hovered around
zero degrees. Not a fit night out for man nor beast. A good night
to be indoors and out of the elements. Yet the hungry must be
fed; the cold, warmed; and the homeless, sheltered. I was living
at St. Francis Inn in the inner city of Philadelphia.

It was my night to go into the side yard and collect the bed
cards. A job I did not relish. I knew I was in for quite a night:
bitter weather; three hundred fifty to four hundred cold, hungry
men; and only thirty-five clean, warm beds. We treated our
guests to a hot, nourishing meal and a hot shower . . . plus a
check for body lice.

SHIVERING HUMANITY
While the children and women were inside the Inn enjoying
their meal, I went outside to collect the hundreds of bed cards.
A sea of shivering humanity greeted me as I pressed through

the crowd. Hundreds of hopeful men thrust their bed cards into my hands. All of them anxious; hopeful!

When the women and children finished their meal, the men came into the dining room. I went to the office and started to sift through the hundreds of bed cards stacked before me. I prayed silently for courage and strength; and proceeded to try and put the older, sicklier men on the top of the pile of cards. I wanted to see to it that they were given beds for the night.

LORD, GIVE ME STRENGTH

What an enormous and perhaps impossible task before me. Lord, give me your strength—now!

When the men finished their meal, I went to the front of the dining room and began to call out their names: bed one: John Jones. Bed two: Mike. . . . and so on down the line. Finally I came to the last man and my heart was racing. I called out the last name, bed thirty-five. All the beds had now been filled.

This was the moment I dreaded. With heart pounding, I announced that the beds were all filled for the night. The room became filled with moaning, groaning, and cursing. Suddenly, one young man ran through the crowd toward me. In the blink of an eye, he clenched his fist and punched me right in the mouth with all his might. I never saw so many stars as I did that night.

MY THREE FRONT TEETH

I stood there in total shock and spit out my three front teeth. They bounced across the tile floor like three little Chiclets. I was stunned. I could not believe what had happened to me. The perpetrator took off out the front door with me in dazed pursuit.

After chasing him for a few blocks through the evening crowd, I lost sight of him, and gave up. I'd never catch him. He won. I lost. God! Did I hurt!

My eyes became moist and my mouth was bleeding profusely as I made my way back to the Inn. St. Francis would have called this PERFECT JOY. That would have been easy for him to say. I was the one who got hit!

I WAS A MESS

As the days passed, I healed physically; but emotionally I was a mess. If I ever see this guy again, I hope I'm within reach of a baseball bat. I became bitter and angry; resentful and hateful. I couldn't let go of it. The anger and negativity became an obsession. I was consumed with it. It interfered with my spiritual life. I struggled to pray. Peace of mind was gone. "Lord, rescue me from the nether world!"

Part of my physical healing was the fact that I had to have my three front teeth replaced. I went to the dentist and as I seated myself in the chair the music in the office played *"I'll Never Smile Again!"* Perish the thought; I certainly hope so!

One day, while doing my duties, one of the brothers told me that there was a gentleman to see me. I went downstairs to meet my visitor. I was shocked; stunned. Surely my eyes were failing me! Standing before me was the guy who decked me.

WHAT DO YOU WANT?

My anger and resentment immediately surfaced as I faced my attacker. Reluctantly, I asked him what he wanted. Was I being called to turn the other check? Had I had enough?

Rather sheepishly, he began to speak. He asked for my forgiveness. He said he was sorry for what had happened. He had lost it that night.

Many nights he was fed, clothed, and sheltered. This particular night he was cold, hungry, and dirty. He needed a warm bed, a hot meal, and a hot shower. He was turned away because of the crowd. He turned to violence. It fell upon me.

He explained his upbringing . . . a good home, hard-working parents, and a belief in Bible teachings; especially forgiveness. That's why he was here . . . to ask forgiveness. What a gift! He extended his hand. I could have refused it, denied forgiveness! Allowed bitterness to keep fueling my life.

Accept the gift! God is so good. God comes to us in many ways; many disguises—through pain, hurt, and brokenness. I learned such a valuable lesson: "to err is human, to forgive . . . divine."

Today I can smile with my new teeth and even chew gum. Pass the Chiclets!

friar Emmet

Silence without Dignity

Sundays were always sleep-in days for me and November 4, 1978, was no different. When I got up, the side street, next to the friary, was already lined with the trucks and buses that brought people to the market. The wide street in front of the church was filled with people buying and selling. Welcome to Bolivia!

Market day is a family day, and parents with their children and venders with every variety of commodity line Avenida Diez y Seis de Julio. There are times when the market is so crowded that walking, even at a slow pace, comes to a standstill because of the congestion.

During the past several days, the people had been celebrating *la fiesta des las Almas* (the feast of All Souls), and this was the last day of the celebration. The streets were more crowded than usual. During this fiesta people visit the cemetery to pray for their dead and bring with them the foods their deceased relatives enjoyed in life. The belief is that the dead return at this time, so the people go to be with them and share with them the food they have brought. An air of somberness pervades and everyone is dressed in black. The priest usually arrives at the cemetery about mid-morning to pray for the dead. It is after his departure that the eating and drinking begin. What had begun as a mournful day turns into a spirited celebration. Heavy drinking continues throughout the commemoration. The people believe the more they drink, the more they will be united with their deceased relatives, at least briefly.

I went to the chapel that Sunday morning, the one day I could count on for an uninterrupted period of prayer and quiet. It was a day of silence that provided me with the opportunity to enter into myself and enjoy undisturbed moments with my God. It was a time of peace, contentment, absolute pleasure, almost as if I were crossing the boundary to eternal stillness. Settled ten minutes, I heard crackling noises coming from the street.

Firecrackers during these celebrations were common, so I thought nothing of it. I tried to resettle myself and opened the

Bible to Job 19:26, *"And from my flesh I shall see God, my inmost being is consumed with longing."*

The crackling (firecrackerlike noise) continued and I heard people screaming and running in the market. Within the next minute Juan burst into the chapel, *Francisco, vete a la clínica inmediatamente!* "Francis, go to the clinic right away!"

Rushing to the clinic, I was bombarded from every direction. Frightened people, injured people, questioning people mobbed me. A quick check found the two treatment rooms filled with wounded. A dead youth lay in a back room. I did not know where to begin. The wounded lay on the floor, huddled on chairs and some walked dazed in circles. *Ayudame!* "Help me!" *Ven aqui!* "Come here!" Two Sisters who were nurses rushed in from the market and told me the awful truth of the moment. A military helicopter passing above the open market fired a machine gun into the immense crowd to instill fear and play sport with human life.

(Several days previous to this Sunday, Bolivia experienced its 187th change of government in 154 years of independence, another military coup. The military leaders specifically chose this time for the coup because they knew the people would be distracted by *la fiesta de las Almas*.)

I quickly assessed the situation and began attending the most serious. The face of a nineteen-year-old youth was swollen and distorted; he was supported against the wall by his father. I touched his jaw, it moved in several directions at the same time. The left side of his mouth was hanging in fragmented pieces covered with dripping blood. I cleaned his mouth and noticed tiny particles of bone clinging to the gauze. His hard palate was fractured too. The bleeding continued. There was no way to stop it. I packed his mouth with gauze and asked a nurse to change it as it soaked up his blood.

His father asked me, *Va a estar bien?* "Will he be all right?" I told him that his son needed further treatment at a hospital in La Paz. The man's face was already distorted with pain. I could not tell him his son would soon be dead. There was a penetrating, questioning look in his eyes. "Why my son? Why this shooting?"

Next, I attended a man who was shot in the right foot. The bullet had gone clear through. There was no heavy bleeding. Some bones seemed broken, but without an X ray I could not be sure. I bandaged his foot. Several ambulatory wounded had bullets still in them. Not knowing the extent of any possible internal injuries, one of the Sisters asked the ambulance driver, who just arrived, to take these patients to the hospitals in La Paz and return for the others.

Next, the Sisters and I attended an eighteen-year-old youth. His left leg was swollen to twice its size. The knee and the thigh were torn open where the bullet had entered. Bleeding profusely, large sections of his thigh muscle were ripped and jagged, and some of the ligaments around the knee were severed. He had lost a lot of blood by the time we got to him. The swelling made application of a tourniquet difficult. We could not apply adequate pressure to diminish the blood flow. The youth was going into shock. One of the nurses gave him an intravenous medication that expanded his blood volume, while the other nurse and I applied a dressing over the large wound. Hardly was it applied when the dressing was soaked with blood. We reinforced the dressing and applied more pressure to the tourniquet. The pressure should have caused considerable pain, but the youth showed no signs of pain. He was in total shock.

Our hands were dripping with blood, the table was streaked with it and large pools spotted the concrete floor. Each stain of blood told a story, carried a unique individual tale and wrote the history that everyone experienced that day. The ambulance returned and took the remaining injured to La Paz. Still with us was the dead youth in the back room. No one had claimed his body.

I left the clinic, and stepping into the street noticed the market was almost totally deserted. A few people were selling things in the doorway of their homes and stray dogs wandered, looking for food left behind. An unusual silence pervaded the air. In spite of the continued firing of automatic weapons, this odd silence kept ringing through the disrupted day. Lively chatter, laughing children, barking dogs had been muffled by the silence of horror.

As I returned home I was stopped by a man who asked me to sign a death certificate for his son. I wanted to see the body. I entered his home, dimly lighted with candles. The body of a fifteen-year-old adolescent lay on the table. His friends said Carlos was a lively football player. He had the ability to kick and run that would put him in the lineup with any professional. That morning while playing football he jumped in jubilation after making a goal, and then a silver dart from the helicopter smashed him to the ground. I prayed with the family, wrote out the death certificate, and left for home. The horror of the football murder, the foreboding scratch of the pen on the death certificate, the stoic wail of the sorrow-stricken women went with me.

As I walked back to the friary everything seemed bleaker than usual to me. At 14,000 feet, trees and flowers find no environment to forge an existence. Homes of adobe brick reflect the same drab color of the earth, no plot of grass refreshes the senses, no flowers scent the air. The sounds and reality of death were all around and even nature could not provide a contrast to give refreshment. What I had hardly noticed before became the blaring silence of eternity. The commemoration of *la fiesta de las Almas* continued.

By mid-afternoon the heavy tank and gun fire of the morning had quieted down, although sporadic rifle fire could be heard. Then came a knock at the friary door. The request of the three men was simple, "Could I attend their wounded relative?" My medical bag seemed heavier than usual. The walk was long, impregnated with that silence, that stillness of eternity I had never experienced before. I chatted lightly with the men, but this terrifying silence invaded our conversation. Even the dogs, usually so full of life, were quiet, aware that something was not normal. We hugged the buildings as we walked to avoid stray bullets.

In the courtyard of the house the women stood in one group, the men in another, between them a man lay on the ground. His face was streaked with dry blood while fresh blood continued to ooze out, into tiny pools on the ground around his head. I found the wound in his head, a bullet hole, the size of my thumb. It told me all I needed to know.

After packing the wound, I told the family the hard truth, the cold reality that penetrates to the bone. For their relative, their friend, life was ebbing. Their silence of hope stuttered through a whimper into a wail. I washed the dying man's face, removed the encrusted blood, cut away his matted hair, and there was the face of youth. That morning Daniel had gone to the market to purchase a few things for his family. Twenty dollars a week would not buy much, but for his wife and three children he did the best he could. While returning home, the gunfire rang from the helicopter. He hugged the ground. Then believing the death machine had completed its sting of terror, he rose. The next round of shooting struck him unconscious.

With his head resting in my arms, I changed the blood-soaked packing. I could not let this man die without the warmth of another human life touching him. In his ears I whispered prayers so he would know on some level that there was still a God who cared, who loved him, and who was waiting for him. Soon his labored breathing faded, then stopped. The wailing of the women diminished, the stonelike stare of the men became rigid and the coldness of this foreboding silence bore further within me. Who next would be struck by this terror of hate, by the discharge of weapon? Who next? Who next?

The remainder of the day was not as demoniac as the morning. That evening I finally had a chance to return to chapel. I needed time to rest, to be alone, to reflect on the events of the day, and above all to pray, to pray for the people, to pray for those who had died. I tried to return to the quiet mood of the morning, but it was always interrupted by the malignant silence that had grown through the course of the day. What happened? Why so many people injured and killed? What need had the military to play sport with human life?

The recollected day choked on terror and death. The escalating eternalized silence witnessed horror. Where would it lead? Death seeks the dignity of tranquility. This day, peace and anguish wrestled. Life still awaited us the living, and another life greeted the dead who had passed into eternity. The pleasured peace of the morning and the pernicious silence of the day danced side by side, seizing me in frustration, but for the moment the hollow, empty stillness that began with the first round of gunfire pervaded.

As I look back on the events of that day in November 1978, it was a day and time of immense transformation for me. One does not go through such an experience without it having a profound impact on one's life.

I remember during the week following that day as rifle and tank fire continued, and I went out to care for the wounded, I would ask myself, "What am I doing here? Is this really where God wants me? What if I get killed? Is it worth it?"

What I came to realize is that I was exactly where God wanted me to be. I was there to be in service to God, and to my sisters and brothers who needed me more than ever. I was there to support, help, care for, and in some small way be the presence of Christ to them as they were the presence of Christ to me; the frightened Christ, the lonely Christ, the wounded Christ.

Even though the events of the day and the days that followed were some of the most horrible that I have ever experienced, it was in the very midst of them that I found God.

friar Francis

* * *

Choices Sublime or Sad Reasons

When I was ordained to the priesthood, my classmates (thirty-six), and I were thrust out into the world where we were put on a pedestal—basically the priest was not seen as human. This was OK if I wanted to hide what I perceived as my not-so-hot or not-so-sure self. I played that game for a while but it was unreal, especially because I knew that I was human.

In the parish there certainly were times when I shook a hand and would like to have kept it, engaged in a passing embrace and would like to have made it more permanent. It was not easy to love everyone and have no one.

FANTASIES

But any fantasies I had on marriage were counteracted by a negative view from the marriage problems that paraded in. On the other hand, it never happened to me that a couple came in and said: "We're so happily married, we'd like to tell you about it!" In time the negative view was balanced out nicely by some Catholic action/marriage support groups (Christian Family Movement, CFM). In that community of young couples there were signs of increasing Christian awareness and service, a lot of laughs, some anger and tears, but always evidence of the real struggle of ongoing relationships and growing families. Maybe the grass was greener there but obviously did not grow without real toil.

"Mircea Eliade once wrote that the frenetic pursuit of the erotic could be seen as a desire for God, for the transcendent, in cultures whose religious forms were dead" (*NCR*, 7/19/91).

In our age, celibacy is patently countercultural; we live in a sensual, erotic time. The *Playboy* philosophy of women as sexual objects, pantingly available, heightens fantasy. The witness value of celibacy by now seems nonexistent. Though recognition is given for other forms of sacrifice. (Remember Joe Namath's knees? How about LT, despite a pulled hamstring, knocking the snot out of some quarterback? Wow!)

SEXUAL SELF-SACRIFICE

But the psychology of sexual self-sacrifice is now so remote to our understanding as to be inaccessible, thanks probably to Freud and Margaret Mead. What is available is the suspicion of neurotic reasons for this choice of life. So you wonder and figure human nature being what it is, there are in most life choices sublime and sad reasons. People marry out of love and also from neurotic needs. Young men become policemen for law and order service, or sometimes for authoritarian bullying. Some doctors and nurses might have an abnormal fear of death. For the celibate, if the sad reasons endure over the sublime ones, he or she better get out. One reason I've heard is that they didn't realize what they were getting into.

CAN'T SAY THAT

I can't say that. When I was ordained basically I knew what I was doing. But what I didn't know was, at times, the real pain this commitment would involve in the long run. In the same breath a young man gets married, basically he knows what he is doing. But what he doesn't know is the struggle and effort and commitment needed to keep that relationship going. A young couple has children; basically they know what they are doing; they welcome them. But what they don't know is the pain and effort and commitment it will take in the long run to grow up with them.

In the whole picture though, there is gain as we grow and mature through all this. At the heart of all love is sacrifice. That is a truism the celibate shares with the married person. I'm convinced that there is as much sacrifice in marriage as in a chosen single life.

friar Claude

* * *

Pedro Is Late

It was my year as principal of a high school in a small rural town in the interior of Brazil. Realizing I was a marshmallow when it came to disciplining (and at age twenty-eight, not too far beyond my own undisciplined years), I was determined to develop the "stone face" of a truly intimidating principal. I was able to practice this almost daily, as each classroom had at least fifty students, and there was a constant procession of students being sent to "see the principal."

One who was in my office everyday was Pedro. He was in the seventh grade, and always late for the first class. When he finally did show up, his shirt was usually ripped or dirty, or he would not be wearing the socks that were part of the school uniform. He never had his homework done, and when I would ask, in my "God the Father" tone of voice, he would just hang his head in silence, or mumble "I don't know." Keeping him after school brought no changes. Notes I sent home to his parents were ignored, or not delivered.

POWER STRUGGLE

About two months into the semester, I noticed that Pedro was not in school at the end of the first period. It was the *ninth* day in a row. I was determined to win this power struggle.

I stormed out of the school and strode down the street, wearing my stone face. Pedro's house was several blocks from the school, on the edge of town. It was a typical mud-brick house with wooden windows, consisting of two rooms. Four sack curtains hung in the front doorway. I called out a greeting, pushed aside the curtains and stepped in. Pedro, as I suspected, was not even dressed for school. What I had not suspected was the scene before me.

Pedro was sitting on the side of the bed, spooning cornmeal into the mouth of an emaciated, wrinkled woman; his mother. Two half-naked, dirty toddlers played on the packed earth floor. Pedro was late for school every day and never did his homework because, as the oldest, he was taking care of four smaller brothers and sisters, getting them ready for school every morning, feeding his bedridden mother, washing the clothes, preparing the rice and beans, and dealing with a father who worked some days and drank the rest of the time. Pedro had never explained the reasons for his lateness out of embarrassment, and so not to shame his parents.

I learned a lot from Pedro: there is a big difference between firm and rigid. But, even more important: every person has a story to tell. They don't always say it in words.

friar Charley

* * *

Paschal Mystery

It was early on Holy Thursday morning. The phone rang, and Terry, a good friend of all the friars, asked if one of the friars would visit her daughter who had just been in an automobile accident. When I arrived at the hospital I found Terry's daughter Tara in the critical care unit. She was lying motionless, flat on her back, with respiratory and IV tubes in place. Her face was bruised, cut and swollen, her hair matted with blood. Fear of aggravating the head injuries Tara had received in the accident prevented the nurses from cleaning her face and hair. The doctor was struggling to determine the source of her internal bleeding, the most immediate and critical problem.

Her parents, Terry and Michael, stood by her bedside. Soon her sisters and brothers arrived. We prayed for the miracle we knew was Tara's only hope. I anointed her with the oil of the sick, and each family member bent over and spoke words of their love for her. Although Tara appeared to be in a coma, we believed in our hearts that she heard our voices and felt our presence.

HELPLESSNESS

The long agonizing vigil with Tara had begun. Two hours earlier she had been driving to the hospital where she worked as a dietitian. Twenty-three years old, so young, so beautiful, so filled with vitality and youthful idealism. The age-old unanswerable question of "why" cried out again for an answer. As we stood by her bed in silence, that terrible feeling of helplessness gripped us. Soon the emergency medical team returned to continue their treatment, so we went to the waiting room and waited, waited, waited. "They also serve who only stand and wait."

Holy Thursday was a very long tension-filled day. The doctors, nurses, and hospital staff were wonderful. They kept Terry, Michael, and the family aware of what was happening, what they intended to do, and called specialists for additional help. Their sense of compassion was a source of strength and hope. Each time they finished their procedure, we returned to her bedside, watched, prayed, and joined our hands with hers. Evening finally arrived, the evening that we would have been gathering to celebrate the Last Supper. Tara remained absolutely still. I looked at the faces of Terry, Michael, and the family. Their expression, their silent anguish must have been a sharing of Mary's experience, Mary's heart as she stood by the cross and helplessly watched her son's life slip away.

LET HER GO

Just before midnight the doctor told us that despite all their effort, all their consultation with specialists, and all the prayers that had been offered, there was no hope. "Then let her go peacefully to God," Terry and Michael said.

Once more we gathered around Tara's bed and prayed together the ritual of the Church commending Tara's soul to God. It was early on Good Friday morning. "Into your hands, O Lord, I commend my spirit."

The doctor who had been present form morning until night, and had worked so tirelessly, then asked Terry and Michael if they would speak privately with hospital authorities about the possibility of donating Tara's vital organs for other people in need. They retired to another room for the discussion, and returned in just a few minutes. They had given permission for the use of any vital organs that would be helpful.

It was almost two A.M. as we walked out of the hospital, into the night, and into a vacant parking lot. It was cold and barren, a place that induced a feeling of numbness beyond tears. We said goodnight and drove home.

Tara's Mass of Christian Burial was celebrated on Easter Wednesday. The newly blessed paschal candle was tall and burning brightly like Tara's spirit. It meant more to me on that day than on any of the forty Easters past. I think others in the church may have felt the same.

TARA'S HEART LIVES

A few weeks later Terry and Michael received a letter telling them of the people who had received organ transplants. A woman who works as a physician had received Tara's heart, and with that a new life. A father of two children had new hope for himself and his family because of Tara's liver. A young diabetic mother with a ten-month-old baby was restored to health by a transplanted kidney and pancreas. A young husband no longer needed dialysis because of a kidney transplant. And someone in danger of blindness would have the miracle of vision restored because of the gift of Tara's eyes. Perhaps all of those rescued lives give new meaning to Jesus' words on that first Holy Thursday, "There is no greater love than this, to lay down one's life for one's friends."

Shortly before he died, Fr. Jack Conway, a priest of the archdiocese of Newark and a hospital chaplain, was asked what he would like his epitaph to say. His answer was: "I have never done any really great things in my life, but I have been present for many great moments." I think that Fr. Jack knew the secret of what it means to be a disciple. I think he knew how to let Christ's wish come true, "that my joy may be yours." As Woody Allen puts it, "Eighty percent of life is just showing up." Location, location, location!

friar Brennan

Saying No/Crossing the Line

For well over a hundred years, the Kensington area of Philadelphia supported a thriving, industrial economy. Fathers got their sons jobs at the plant and saw to their transition to responsible adults. The (mostly) Catholic churches and schools flourished. But then over a period of twenty years (the 1950s to the 1970s) the factories moved south, for cheaper, nonunion labor, driven by the economic imperative of stockholder/owner profits. Germany and Japan put their workers first and it seems, they have a stronger social fabric than we do. So many fathers without jobs turned to drink and had little control over their sons and daughters who turned to drugs.

BEST-PROTECTED SLUMS

Philadelphia magazine called the Kensington section "a white slum." Our soup kitchen, St. Francis Inn, served mostly whites until government cuts closed down a Salvation Army facility north of us. Something had to go with the military/weapons priority of the Reagan years and the cities went down; and the few government programs still running (Model Cities), had no economic center to build around.

The military imperative said we needed more missiles to protect our way of life, to protect our cities. So what do we have but the world's best-protected slums. The cities are no longer seen as the locus of culture and ideas, and are left to battle the perception that they deserve their fate.

For all of the above reasons I wanted to register dissent. There's a story from the book *Bread and Wine* by Ignazio Silone about an antifascist in Italy during the 1930s. When Mussolini's Italy declared war on Ethiopia, the man runs out and chalks up "No" on all the buildings. Those hiding him object, but he says: "One person shouting 'No' is enough to break the unanimity."

That "no" for me first found expression with a young-adult charismatic prayer group in Northeast Washington, D.C. They continued protesting after the Vietnam War. In 1980 there was the largest demonstration in years at the Pentagon, protesting the arms race. We intended to block the doors and get arrested. We took up positions by the doors and sat down. The well-disciplined police moved in, cleared a large set of doors, and ignored the rest of us.

As the afternoon wore on, we drifted away. One of the members of Dan and Phil Berrigan's group asked me: "Weren't you with the ones getting arrested?" What could I say but: "Many are called, but few are chosen."

A scary group in the protest, the "Spartacus Youth Brigade" I think they called themselves, were aching for a confrontation with the cops. They taunted them with violent language and gestures. Bad enough risking arrest, I didn't want my head broken, too. After that we worked more closely with Sojourner's, a Protestant, liberal evangelical community that put out an excellent magazine with the same name.

Their demonstrations were preceded by much prayer and discernment, and they organized "affinity groups" so that the participants were on the same page. One of the protests (in 1983 I think) stressed "Life." Different affinity groups were dispatched to the State Department (against the administration's Central American policy), the White House (against the arms race), the Supreme Court (against abortion), the Russian embassy (against the Afghanistan invasion), and the South African embassy (against apartheid).

PLASTIC HANDCUFFS

I joined the last group as I was involved in the corporate responsibility level petitioning corporations to stop propping up apartheid by their presence. (Now we are trying to get them back in the country.) We "crossed the line" and police arrested us, putting plastic handcuffs on. A paddy wagon pulled up (it's usually a bus), and we moaned. These are very cramped, and you have to sit bent over, six people to each side of a steel cylinder. My latent claustrophobia welled up and I nearly panicked . . . and I prayed some desperate prayer. Immediately a wonderful peace descended on me. It was beautiful.

Art Laffin, one of the protesters, groaned: "the last time I was in one of these, it was a couple of hours." Even with this euphoric feeling, I thought, "No way!" It was a couple of hours before we were out of the wagon and that presence never left me. It was beautiful.

friar Claude

The Mule's Fault

Have you ever gotten some bad, negative news? And your reaction was, "Hey, that's the best news I've had in a long time." That happened to me recently. A neurologist told me, "Your medical results definitely show that you have MS, multiple sclerosis." That was great, absolutely terrific news.

HERE I AM

Let met tell you my story. In October 1965, I went to Bolivia to be a missionary. I was a young priest, ready to go tirelessly to the poor in Bolivia. I remember getting off the plane. In La Paz, excitedly seeing the Bolivian people, and the thought came, "OK, everyone, here I am."

It didn't take long for the problems to begin. I suddenly found out that I didn't know Spanish. Sure, I had studied some, but the people spoke so fast I couldn't understand what they were saying. That was my first frustration. And the customs of the people! "They certainly are different"! And the food! Have you ever heard of Montezuma's revenge?

MY PRAYER

It was at that time I learned a prayer that is still with me. Now I say it at least several times each day: "Lord, please help me to remember that nothing is going to happen to me today that you and I together can't handle." I realized that sitting around complaining was not the way. I had to do my part. If anything was beyond my capabilities, the Lord would be there to carry me through. So, I began on a process that was going to see me end up learning Spanish, and accepting and loving the customs of the people. But, Montezuma continued to have a smile on his face.

The day came for me to go to my parish. It was a twelve-hour jeep ride from La Paz to a town called Charazani, eleven thousand feet above sea level. Waiting for me were two Franciscans who were older than my fifty-two-year-old father. I thought they'd be old men, but it turned out that we became one of the best families I've ever lived in.

BY FOOT OR MULE

The jeep road ended in Charazani. From then on, all traveling had to be done on foot or by mule. I got to be pretty good at loading up cargo on one mule, and I riding the other. Of course it was a real struggle to learn how to ride a mule, but I got to be quite good at it. I even began to speak another language, Quechua, which the people of that region spoke.

Then the fatal day came. Of all things, I had a tremendous fall from the mule, I landed on solid rock. It was obvious to me that nothing was broken, so I just struggled on for a week, visiting several towns. Upon arriving at Charazani, I just chalked it up as a missionary experience and said, "well, that's the way it goes." I never bothered to get checked out for any possible damage.

About six months later I started having frequent muscle spasms in my arm and leg. I was due for my stateside vacation and the thought came, "this is a great chance to check out what the problem is." After some days of extensive tests in a Miami hospital, the doctors came to my room and said, "We just can't seem to figure out what exactly is the problem; we think it may be the beginning stages of multiple sclerosis." I really didn't even know what MS was, so I just forgot about it, and didn't tell anyone what the doctors had said.

After a great three-month stay with relatives in Miami, I returned to Bolivia. Eventually I became the superior of the American Franciscan group. Several years later I was elected president of the Bolivian Franciscan federation, which was comprised of two hundred sixty Franciscans from eight countries.

CONSTANT TINGLING

About this time, I started feeling strange sensations in my arms and legs. There was a numbness, a loss of feeling, and a constant tingling all over my body. To me, there was just one explanation—the fall from the mule! These sensations persisted for the rest of my time in Bolivia.

Eventually I returned to the states to do ministry. Many tests had been done over the years to find out the cause of my symptoms, but no explanations could be determined. Clearly there was just one solution—just live with the numbness, the tingling, the loss of feeling, even though they gradually became more pronounced.

NOT YOUR FAULT

A few complications arose in my ministry. For example, at Mass, hosts fell out of my hands as I distributed Communion. I'd tell the people about my accident in Bolivia. "Please don't be upset," I'd say, "If a host falls to the floor; it's not your fault: and, it's really not my fault. It's the mule's fault." I remember what happened when I gave a mission in Augusta, Georgia. At the time of the anointing of the sick, the people lined up to receive the sacrament. I approached the first person and all of a sudden the oil stock fell from my hand and rolled a short distance. I picked it up, approached the young man, and again it fell from my hands. I picked it up and apologized profusely. He smiled and said, "That's okay, Father; it's that darned mule's fault."

It was at that mission in Augusta, Georgia, that a doctor heard my story about the fall from the mule. He approached me and suggested an MRI for the next day.

Dr. Binet saw something on the MRI that had to be studied, so he gave me the name of a doctor in Tampa. After another MRI in Tampa, after blood tests, a spinal tap, and I don't know what else, the doctor said to me, "it sure looks like you have multiple sclerosis; but it can't be, because you're too old for that."

That statement came as a shocker to me! It was the first time anyone ever said that I was too old for something. Suddenly I realized the years were passing by quickly. He sent me to another neurologist, who put me through many tests again. When all was completed he said, "there's no doubt about it, you have multiple sclerosis." I answered, "no, because the other doctor said I'm too old for it." "When MS started," he replied, "you were not too old." For me that was like a revelation—that makes sense! MS normally appears between the ages of twenty and forty. I was thirty-five years old when those muscle spasms appeared in Bolivia. I was thirty-seven when the numbness, tingling, and other symptoms began. I'm now sixty years old and they say I have the chronic progressive type of MS. It has developed very slowly, but it has developed.

GREATEST NEWS

Strange as it may seem, when the doctor gave his conclusion: "you have MS," it was the greatest news! At least I now know what my problem is. It's no longer necessary to guess and wonder. Since finding out what my illness is, I have joined a self-help group of people with MS. It has been extremely interesting to find out the symptoms of MS, to meet persons coping with it, and to see how others so willingly, and faithfully, look to the Lord for strength. The persons I met have been a real inspiration for me.

I'm fortunate because MS has developed in me very slowly over the years. Sure, I can't do what I could do twenty years ago or even five years ago; but who can?

NOTHING WE CAN'T HANDLE

There's no doubt that the Lord has been with me all my life, in Bolivia, in the Bronx, in Florida now, and everywhere I've been. God is with me right now. As I prayed before and as I pray now: "Lord, help me to remember that nothing is going to happen to me today that you and I together can't handle."

One last thing—after blaming everything on that poor mule for so long, I wish I could tell that poor animal, "I'm sorry, it really wasn't your fault."

friar Marty

* * *

Jackie O Is on This Plane

I couldn't believe it! My friend Thomas told me he saw Jackie Kennedy Onassis coming back from the ladies room. We were at La Guardia Airport, waiting for our plane to visit our friend Stuart in Palm Beach, Florida. I *had* to walk over to the huge window, making believe I wanted to look out, while what I really wanted was to slyly turn my head around to get a good look at the first row of seats in the waiting room, where we thought *she* was sitting.

I started practicing how I would address her. In my deepest, and I have to say, sexiest voice, I kept repeating to Thomas: "Hi Jackie!" and, "Hello Mrs. Kennedy!" *Which* name did she want? Thomas and I were two little kids laughing our rear ends off!

We wondered, was she going to their famous beach-front mansion in Palm Beach? She must be! Why else would she be here? She had to be! She was! I couldn't believe it!

We purchased our tickets separately, so unfortunately our seats were not together. I happened to be next to a very nervous woman, who was talking a mile a minute, especially during take off! I was in regular clothes. We were on vacation! I usually don't advertise who I am when on vacation, but I thought I'd try and comfort this poor woman.

DON'T WORRY
So I said, with tank top and shorts on: "Don't worry, you're in good hands. I may not look like it, but I'm a Catholic priest and Jackie O is on this plane. They'd never let *this* plane crash!" She seemed to feel a tiny bit better, and got to talking.

TWO DIRECTIONS
Whenever somebody finds out you're a priest, they usually can go in two directions . . . naming every priest they have ever met in their life, or feel like they have to talk about religion!—why I guard my identity when on vacation. I'm on vacation! Here we go.

She was telling me that she had just come from a funeral of a close relative in West Milford, New Jersey. Usually you don't know anybody or anywhere people are talking about. But this parish of St. Joseph's was right next to where I was stationed, in Pompton Lakes! I couldn't believe it!

She went on saying how nice the priest was. So warm, so consoling to the family. Seemed to make everybody feel good on this unpleasant occasion! I asked if it was a tiny little church? She said yes. Were they Franciscans? She didn't know. I knew. It was one of our parishes!

She described the priest. Sounded like someone I knew. I asked if his name was Fr. Mychal Judge? She said yes!

NEVER SO PROUD
I was never happier to be a Franciscan! Never so proud to be a friar! I was never so proud of one of my friars! That was a greater treat than being on the same plane with Jackie!

I was truly blessed. In Admonition 191, we hear the words of St. Francis: "Blessed is that friar who is no more elated at the good which the Lord says and does through him, than that which the Lord says and does through anybody else." What a treat.

friar Kevin

* * *

There, but for the Grace of God

Every night he slowly comes up Kensington Avenue. On two steel crutches, dragging his two very crippled legs behind him and comes in to eat at St. Francis Inn. One evening after the meal he was sitting outside and I began talking to him, and then Danny revealed how he was injured.

He was in Vietnam, a young healthy man in his early twenties. He was out on patrol one night with his buddies and he stepped on a land mine. It wasn't the type that explodes out, it exploded up . . . and shattered the lower half of his body. He woke up three days later in a hospital in Saigon. They were going to amputate both legs. Then they decided to try to save them. He was in a hospital in Vietnam, in the Philippines, and in Hawaii for a total of two years. He had fourteen major operations. "Look, Brother," he said as he rolled up his pant legs. "I have more plastic in my legs than I have bones." There was a mass of crisscrossed scars on all sides up and down both legs. It looked terrible.

But it wasn't only his legs that were shattered. It was also his mind. The Vietnam experience took its toll on his mind. While in the hospital those two years, Danny became dependent on the pain killers and the drugs. When he was released, he turned to alcohol and street drugs. He is still hooked. His life is a shambles. He barely survives. Here it is some twenty-three years later and Danny is still losing the Vietnam War.

WINNING THE LOTTERY

I had a lot to think about at prayer that evening. I am the same age as Danny. I too lived through the draft, the protests, the agony of the late 1960s. Back then they had the draft lottery. Every young eligible man was issued a draft lottery number.

What if the person who drew Danny's number turned their head to cough or clear their throat, and their hand moved an inch to the left and *my* number was drawn!

It could have been *me* who was on patrol. It could have been me who stepped on the land mine. I could easily be in the line at the soup kitchen tonight and Danny could be a Franciscan serving me. There but for the grace of God . . . .

friar Michael

* * *

No TGIF for Me

I was twenty-one-years old, a young Franciscan novice in Lafayette, New Jersey, St. Raphael's Novitiate, where I was to spend one year of my life, beginning my life as a friar minor. We were the last class that would be there and have a traditional novitiate . . . the last of the old, 1968–69.

LAST CLASS

Because we would be the last class there, we did things a little differently. In the olden days a novice could not leave the novitiate for one year and a day. Since our novice master, Daniel O'Rourke, knew it was his swan song, he let up a little. We had regular jobs on Saturdays, which we had to obtain on our own initiative, like everyone else. And for which we got paid. This was the beginning of the Church opening up to the world, and our witnessing by working among the people, also our staying grounded in reality. I worked in Sussex Tank with Dennis Marcom, where they made septic tanks and other things that needed welding.

MY MISSION

We also had apostolates, works of charity. This I did on Fridays. My mission was to go to the local mental hospital, Greystone State Hospital. Along with six other novices we would drive forty-five minutes in the van to spend an hour and a half on the wards of a state hospital. It was scary to say the least.

FLIRTING

Because we wore our Franciscan habits, some of the men thought we were women and made passes at us. We had no facial hair back then. Others would cling to you out of desperation. Some would say the same nonsense every week, to every person that came along. No one really told us what to do. Just give them God's love! And how do I do that here?

I would attempt to go to each individual in a ward that had perhaps two hundred men scattered throughout, some in beds, some in the day rooms, some walking around. It was so frustrating. Where to begin? How to help?

One man asked every week if I could help him. Many years ago he worked for a major electric company, which brought the unions into upstate New York. He claims that he has been punished every second of every minute, every minute of every hour, every hour of every day by receiving electromagnetic impulses that paralyze him, and keep a thick coating on his tongue, every minute of every day! He was one example. Every week he would show me his thick coating on the tongue.

STRAPPED IN

Another man was strapped into his wooden lawn chair, an Adirondack chair that had thick armrests. His arms were tied with thick cords. A nurse told me he was tied like that because he would always be trying to put his fingers either in his mouth, or as they told me, in his rear end. He thought for some reason that he should always be going to the bathroom.

WASTING MY TIME?

Well, every week I went to this man. I touched his hand and his face. He never talked. I said; "God loves you." I thought I was wasting my time, but I went up to him, touched him, and said those wonderful words of the Good News every dreadful week. Talk about kenosis, this was a total service without any hope of success. We drove home every week exhausted and totally drained, perhaps sharing some funny stories, but always wiped. Who told us ministry would be fun?

MAN UNBOUND

Till one day, as I came into the ward, I saw my tied up man unbound. I was shocked. I was scared! What is going to happen? I was afraid. I spent a few moments with the electromagnetic man till I looked up and who comes over to me, but my "unbound man." He came right up to me like I was his best friend, like he knew me forever. Didn't say a word. He grabbed a magazine, then held it on his hip, placing it in between himself and me, put his arm around my waist. He then accompanied me throughout the whole ward going to each person with me, never saying a word, but never leaving my side. I was in shock. I couldn't believe it.

ROAD TO HOPE

This was one of those rare moments in ministry that told me all the time you put in sometimes does indeed make sense, and may indeed bear fruit. All those seemingly useless gestures sometimes are a road to hope for the minister as well as to the one ministered to, even though you may never know it. So, do your good deeds with love and have hope! God will one day surprise you with some joy!

BAMBOO

I read somewhere once that a seed for a bamboo shoot takes about three years of daily water and sun without ever showing any signs of growth. It needs that time and that nourishment. But after that it sprouts ten to twenty feet or so, all at once. As Mother Teresa says: "We are not called to be successful, but to be faithful." Thank you Lord, for sometimes letting us feel successful. She may not need that, but I do. All glory be to you!

friar Kevin

5

The Joy of Your Help

Give me once again, the joy of your help;
with a spirit of fervor sustain me!
Psalm 51:14

Goodness, Dearie

I have had some "touches" of God's possessive, consummate
love. One occasion stands out. As a young priest I was praying/
meditating one morning and something more than a feeling of
all-embracing love came into me. "Every fiber of my being"
would not describe it. It lasted a few minutes, and I did not
want to come down. It was the highest high, like the apostles
on the mountain with Jesus (Matthew 17:1–9).

Reflecting on this later, I went in the wrong direction, figuring
it was approval, ratification of all I was doing. It was almost as
if I didn't have to progress further. Not so.

THE GOODNESS TEST

A couple of studies maintain that about one out of three people
has had one or more significant spiritual experience. Does this
mean they are better than the next person, that they passed
a "goodness" test or something and God rewards them?
No, I believe God deals with each one of us uniquely, not
comparatively.

St. Thérèse of Lisieux and St. Peter Canisius, it seems, never
had any sensible experience of God. Jesus said to doubting
Thomas: "Blessed are they who have not seen and yet believe"

(John 20:29). The old time comedienne Mae West showed up at a nightclub and gave her fur wrap to the hatcheck girl revealing a diamond pendant. The hatcheck girl said: "Goodness, what a beautiful diamond!" Mae West replied: "Goodness, dearie, had nothing to do with it."

There is no goodness test with God; God loves us, accepts us just the way we are. But God loves too much to leave us there.

friar Claude

* * *

Saturday Night at the Seminary

Shortly after the October bus tour, another seminarian, Tom, and I were walking around the lake in the cool of a Saturday evening. Were we remembering past Saturday nights on the town and contrasting them with the almost monastic quiet and sober quality of our new life? I am not certain, but something set us up for the farce that followed.

A grubby old pickup truck suddenly invaded our recollection by emerging from a wooden area near the lake where no automobile path existed. Our first reaction was fear—the two powerful rough-looking guys were out to celebrate Saturday night by beating up two goodie-goodie little Franciscan seminarians before continuing their riotous night of drinking! Though they startled us by coming from nowhere onto the property, they seemed, nevertheless, quite calm and unagitated as they stepped out of the truck. Tom approached them to inform them that there are roads that lead on and off the Seminary property and wondered why they had chosen such a novel approach through the woods.

LOOKING FOR GIRLS

Since I was a good ten feet away from the conversation, I do not know to this day if they ever answered the question. All I know is that Tom came back to me and whispered: "I think these guys don't know that this is a seminary. They think it is a regular college and they're looking for girls, for one of them asked if I had seen any decent-looking 'night walkers.'" Sensing that I needed to take charge of this situation, I assumed my Brooklyn "cool" macho stance and walked over to these two mistaken townies. In a commanding voice, I said: "Listen, buddy, you and your friend are in the wrong place. This is not a coed college. There are no girls here, so, if you are looking for some exciting action, you better throw your gears into reverse and head out of here." I wanted to be perfectly clear regarding the seminary, as well as to suggest strongly to remove themselves from the property.

NIGHT CRAWLERS

The guy who looked totally puzzled spoke calmly: "I don't know what you're talking about. For years we have come here in the evening to look for some *night crawlers*. We ain't looking for women. Have you seen any night crawlers out this evening?"

First, I smiled inwardly and almost laughed that my companion had heard "night walkers" instead of night crawlers, and understood night walkers to be street walkers (read *prostitutes*). Oh, my, how fear and simple ignorance can sure be funny at times!

One further part of this simple farcical story. Being a city-slicker myself and a nonfisherman, I didn't know what a night crawler was either! Not wishing to compound the weird first impression these townies were getting from two of the "best and brightest" Franciscan students, I immediately spoke eloquently and rapidly about the various species of night crawlers and how the lake, streams, and rich soil of our campus were the ideal environment for attracting healthy, decent looking night crawlers. We gently coaxed them to their truck and left them with words of comfort and hope: we are sorry that we could not be of greater help to them tonight, but will ask the entire student body to keep their eyes peeled for the sight of any night crawlers.

After the two thoroughly confused townies and their truck disappeared in the woods, my companion, Tom, remarked that he was surprised and impressed that I knew so much about night crawlers. For good reason, we changed our walk time to early afternoon and were never again night walkers!

friar Daniel

* * *

Never So Stretched!

It was a hot summer September Thursday evening, 1990. I was on my way home to my parish in New Jersey, after taking my day off at Point Lookout, Long Island, where the friars own a small bungalow. Any of us can go to rest there and refresh our bodies and spirits, which I often do, because it's close to my sister Ronnie's house, and my brother John's. I was to begin duty at 9 P.M. back at St. Mary's in Pompton Lakes. Fr. Charlie asked me to take his place, to start early, the night before. "Duty" meant being around and available for any emergencies, or it meant being the "beeper keeper."

Traffic on the Cross Bronx Expressway was a nightmare as usual, and so I was running late. Usually it didn't matter, there were seldom real emergencies. But I said "I better call after I cross the George Washington Bridge from one of those gas stations, just in case." Marie Wyble, our night secretary, answered and said "Yes, there is an emergency. Three boys from Pompton Lakes High School football team were in a tragic accident on their way home from practice. Their jeep rolled over and two of them were thrown from the car, Angelo Caliente and Bobby Lane, and one other guy whom I did not know. Bobby Lane is in critical condition at Newark trauma unit. There have been kids here all day, in the office and now there are about fifty of them in the church. You are the only one they want to see and talk to."

Oh boy! What a way to end a relaxing day off. I took a deep breath, felt my chest tighten, and drove home to face the music. As soon as I got to the church, I just went in, as I was, tank top and bathing suit. I knew they wouldn't mind. All I could do was just embrace them. Truly had very little to say. You can only imagine the scene. The teenagers stood around in small huddles, weeping, sometimes praying. After about an hour of high anxiety, I lead whoever was there in some prayer. A long day for all.

SHOULD I GO TO NEWARK?

Now it was 10:45 P.M. Should I go in, put my habit on, and go down to Newark to see Bobby Lane? I agonized over that decision. Could it wait till morning? A forty-five minute ride to Newark, the car stealing capital of the world, at 11:30 P.M. on a hot summer night? I couldn't rest. I had to go! I think the kids really wanted me to go. One of those times I practiced kenosis. I went.

What a sad, but still hopeful situation encountering Joan and John Lane, Bobby's parents, whom I never met before. We priests don't always have the magic words. I dread walking into these situations. My dread however began at the GWB! I knew what was ahead of me. I knew what the next few days would be. Why couldn't I have been on vacation where I could not be called or reached? Believe me, if I could have run away from the pain I was to encounter, I would have. There is nothing more awkward than trying to be a priest, trying to give comfort to perfect strangers who are filled with hundreds of feelings of dread, anger, fear, and deep despair. Looking into the tired red eyes of Bobby's mom who was a nurse, I could tell she was very worried. Bobby was in a coma, and they weren't sure exactly what condition he was in.

I had gotten to know Bobby a bit just the year before. I nearly left him back for flunking his confirmation requirements. But I had him do extra make-up things like "going to Mass, and giving me a report of his impressions of the homily, and the like." So, I met with him a few times, which I usually don't do with each of our high school sophomores preparing for the sacrament. Bobby was a charmer! He charmed me. It was so sad seeing him lie there on that stretcher. I felt useless there that night. Helpless, but glad I went.

The next morning I had the 7:30 A.M. parish Mass in the prayer room. I saw about twenty kids who actually squeezed into the room that fits a usual twenty-five on a daily basis. Susie Parker and Joey Compel, who had brought most of the kids the night before, told me that lots of them wanted to come to church today. By the time 7:30 Mass was over, there were a hundred high school students of all religions who wanted to come to church to "pray for Bobby."

THEIR OWN MASS?

Could they have *their own* Mass? Already emotionally and physically exhausted from the night before, I groaned inwardly, and previewed in my mind the coming attractions of the next few very, very heavy days, but how could I refuse . . *teenagers* requesting to have a Mass? So, over to the church we go for Mass #2 for the teenagers. It wasn't too bad, because they still had hope, and they thought their prayers would help Bobby. What to say? "Lord please be with me, say something to their hearts through me, please use me in some small way for these hurting, young, fragile adolescents. My heart aches for them." Angelo, I would see that day at St. Joe's in Paterson. Thank God, other than getting banged up, he would be all right. The other boy was even less hurt, but badly shook up. Bobby was the one everybody loved and whom everybody was worried about.

I was so proud of Susie, Joey, Mike Pagano, Kevin Brandt. These were our confirmed St. Mary's teenage-parishioners who knew where they could bring their aching friends. Everyone was always welcomed at St. Mary's. It really was the whole town's parish. I was so pleased that they thought I could be of some help to them. Just knowing they could come comforted me. They would not be greeted by strange self-righteous, judgmental priests and staff at *this* Catholic church. And this wasn't the only time we saw these pain-racked young people. I guess they did notice that I cared. Even though being their adolescent cool selves who most often tried to ignore that they knew me at their basketball, football, baseball games, that I tried to get to as often as I could, I guess somewhere it did register in those sometimes "from-another-planet" teenage minds, that I was there for them. They did notice. Nice surprise.

The other friars, Charley and Bill, Sister Arlene, and other members of the staff were equally concerned. How could we not? The whole town was in this!

HOW MUCH LORD?

After the Mass came the question, "Can we come back tonight to church?" How much angst can I deal with? Lord, get me out of here! How much can I take? This is already a marathon, and it's only two days old! And now I'm going to have to start dealing with tough pain and impossible feelings and questions, and start addressing them. I'm the adult, I'm the priest, the man of God they have come to trust, listen to and lean on.

How big can my heart be, Lord? How much do you and they want? I'm stretched already and exhausted. OK Jesus! With you, I'll keep going! It is you who are my strength and theirs. Let me remember that. Kenosis!"

"OK kids, come back tonight. The church will be open all day. We usually closed it at 5 P.M. At 7:30 we'll get together and pray." Over three hundred teenage, sad, drawn faces showed up that night with other concerned friends and parents. I remember repeating to them words of wisdom I'd heard along the way, simple things like: "Keep breathing! *You* are not dead. You must eat! Please keep living." Teenage emotions can bury them into despair, and feed on morbid negativity.

ACT NORMAL!

Other words came to mind to say: "Please *act* normal, even if you don't feel it. Sometimes you have to act normal, and it will get you through till you feel normal again!" "Go to football practice! Go to school! Be gentle and patient with each other and everyone else! You're not yourselves. Act normal." They were feeling guilty because someone else was lying in a coma. They wanted to do something about it to help. They were dealing with the most difficult lesson of life . . . that we can't change everything . . . we're not in control. They were feeling guilty for being alive! Why Bobby? And not someone else?

I tried to stick some theology in there about hope, and address very delicately their questions, such as, "Why did God let this happen?" But to tell you the truth, I only tried to listen, to be with them as best I could, to let them know that the church is with them, that Jesus cares. I did very little preaching, even though this would be one of the most reachable and teachable moments of each of their young lives. I had to walk the tightrope of *what* to say and how to say it. "Jesus, please be with me! Say what you want to through me! Use me! Kenosis!" I was a very important and real contact to help many of them get through this, almost like a border guard, to assist each one in making this treacherous crossing. Somehow I dreaded the final outcome of what I would have to say if Bobby died. Then I'd have to pull out everything I had . . . theology and all. Right now I was being the welcomer and the nurturer, yet the gentle nudger, not allowing them to be swallowed up in this paralyzing grief, this shocking numbness, this confining inertia.

The next days were like a roller coaster, hope one day for Bobby, then all hope of recovery gone. It was a very tiring nightmare, which the whole town was hoping to wake up from its fright one day, wishing it only was a bad dream.

I was getting to become friends with the Lane family. Not exactly friends, but they knew me, all the friars, and all the team at St. Mary's was pulling for them. There were both heroic and grateful.

EVERYBODY'S BOBBY

The frightful day arrived. Our Bobby, now everybody's Bobby, died. There was some comfort to the family in knowing that good healthy organs of Bobby would continue to go on living in grateful bodies in many states in this union. Somehow Bobby would go on living physically, almost as much as he would in the hearts of everyone in Pompton Lakes, New Jersey, for a long, long time. Boy! Was this exhausting. Now we almost felt guilty that it was over. Yes, there was a sad sense of some relief. A town that was "on hold" could now begin to go on living again.

Next to my own father's funeral, this was perhaps to be the most challenging funeral ever to preach at and to preside over, much less *celebrate*. Every student in Pompton Lakes High School would be there with all their friends and family. We had all gone through so much with Bobby, and now was the time to say thank-you to God for the memories of this great beloved life-giving young man, and to tearfully say good-bye.

As I began my homily, we all chuckled how much Bob would have loved all this attention, and how he would have liked to have all his friends together in one place, especially in church. We had to laugh to break the grief. We sang all those songs we try to sing to remind us of hope and resurrection: "Be Not Afraid"; "On Eagles' Wings"; "Be with Me, Lord."

BOBBY'S OWN WORDS

The best and only words that hadn't been said yet, were what I thought would work the best. I'd quote from Bobby's make-up papers he wrote, which I still had. I was glad I still had them.

They would give us all help and hope. He wrote to me in a letter form, his exact words and spelling:

> Father,
>   Easter Sunday Mass was about resurrection of Christ on the Holy Sunday. I thought that Jesus' rebirth was like a rebirth in myself. This is the first Mass I was at in a long time, and I learned I still loved Jesus and that he was still alive inside me.

and about another Sunday Mass:

> This Sunday's Mass I was remember that not just on Easter Sunday should I think of Jesus, ᴗᴗ ᵈld think of him all the time. I learned that every day is his day and not to let the Spirit of Jesus within me dissipate.
>
>   Your son,
>   Robert Lane

Now can you see why I agreed to confirm him? Bobby would not have written something he did not mean. We only knew the funny Bobby. In those few short visits with him I got to know somebody was inside those funny bones.

I told all the teenagers how proud of them I was. That we all were. We were so happy that they knew they could come "however they were" to St. Mary's. The doors will continue to be open as we go through the future together. They must keep breathing! Keep living! They didn't die! It will be challenging, but we see how we can get through if we go through together, and with our Lord Jesus. The boys in Bobby's fraternity gave a marvelous testimony and tearful good-bye to their beloved frat brother. There wasn't a dry eye in the church.

If you've ever been the preacher at an event like this, it was one to remember. The church was packed to the rafters. You'd know what an awesome moment and responsibility this would be to have a word to say that people could hang on to. I pray they all heard one. After the casket was put in the hearse, I walked up the side aisle to the back sacristy, wanting to run again and hide from the deep grief and weight I myself was feeling. As I entered the security of the sacristy behind the altar, I just sobbed, sobbed, and sobbed. I remember Alma Banta saw me and gave me her eyes of deep understanding and respectful reverence. I appreciated.

The ride to the cemetery and the burial was what the whole day had been . . . a feeble attempt to be with young people as they struggle with the reality of the death of a friend and perhaps their own finiteness. I have never felt so stretched in every possible human way in my entire life! It was over. And I had that fatigue that sleep can't even relieve. I didn't want to see anybody. After the family reception at the Elks Hall which I tried my best to be present to, I had to politely take my leave, and give everyone else their permission to "try and get back to normal" although that would take a very long time for most.

I remember the thought and the feeling of never being so stretched in my entire being in so many ways, at such intensity, for so long. And yet it is one of the moments I was most happy to be a priest and a friar in my entire life! I was just so pleased that my young friends knew they could come to me, and that I could be there with them, and for them.

CITIZEN OF THE MONTH

One of my greatest honors was to be recognized as "citizen of the month" by the local paper, under the title article that read "Father Kevin helps people of Pompton. We salute you!" One of the exaggerated statements made in the article, which I will share with you, because it's one of the nicest things that have ever been said about me, true or not: "trying to describe Father Kevin Cronin of St. Mary's, it seems, is like trying to describe love itself. Ask anyone who knows him!" All I know is that I never tried so hard to love as I did that week. And I never felt happier to be a Franciscan priest. It made me think of the words on my first Mass booklet, recorded somewhere in the writings of Thomas Merton:

AFRAID OF LOVE?

If you are afraid of love, never become a priest, never say Mass. The Mass will draw down upon your soul a torrent of interior suffering which has only one function, to break you wide open, and let everybody in the world into your heart. When you begin to say Mass, the Spirit of God awakes like a giant inside you and bursts the locks of your own private sanctuary. If you say Mass, you condemn your soul to the torrent of a love that is so vast and so insatiable that you will never be able to bear it alone.

That love is the love of the heart of Jesus burning within your own miserable heart, and bringing down upon you the huge weight of his pity for all the sinners of the world.

Up until that point I had never felt the reality of those words written so idealistically on my program in September 1974. Yes, never so stretched, never loved so much. "You needed me" as the song goes, and my dear friends I was happy to be there as your servant and priest. And with tears in my eyes even now as I write, thank you for calling me to such a great love!

friar Kevin

* * *

Grumpy Ol' Self

I think most people have some defining period in their lives. For some it might simply be "high school hurts" that they never get over. The defining moment might be more than personal and involve national and political factors. The World War II generation and the Vietnam veterans look at themselves and the country with different lenses.

HARSH AND DREADFUL LOVE

For myself an important part of my life and priesthood was my time in Philadelphia. Along with Franciscan sisters and scores of dedicated volunteers, our Province of Franciscans runs a large soup kitchen, night shelters, and thrift shops in inner city Philadelphia (Lower Kensington section.) After eight years in Washington, D.C., working and protesting on different levels of social action, I made a move in downward mobility to St. Francis Inn, Philadelphia in 1982 (to 1987).

It was down and dirty with the poor. There are many and varied emotions in this ministry: frustration and anger when we get conned and ripped off by some. Although this bothers me less because I can't call the money mine. Helplessness: when at our night shelter there is literally no more room at the Inn, and your "no" could mean the person(s) you face might die in the dark winter's night. Dorothy Day often quoted Dostoevski: "Love in action is harsh and dreadful when compared to love in dreams."

I was celebrating the afternoon Mass for the staff and volunteers. After communion during the meditation time I was building mountains out of molehills. I was not looking forward to the coming week's schedule and especially that night when it was my turn in the men's night shelter.

MARIE'S WORD

Then Marie, one of the stalwart volunteers, broke the silence: "I have a word for someone here." She quoted the first verse of the fourteenth chapter of St. John's Gospel: "Do not let your hearts be troubled. Trust in God still, and trust in me." The dejection immediately lifted from me and I realized I was privileged to serve the "least ones" whom Jesus went out to in a special way.

I went over to the shelter that night with a different outlook and a renewed sense of mission. Some of the old-timers even noticed my change of attitude. They said I wasn't "my usual grumpy ol' self."

friar Claude

* * *

Nicknames

I like to give nicknames. I like to get them. I think they are fun! They can be ways of showing endearment to an individual. They can also be a way of picking up on a particular trait of a person, which we or they find amusing, reveling in that trait or kidding the other person about it.

My classmate and good friend, friar John Hogan, whom I call "Hogie," is one of the funniest friars I know. He's great at giving nicknames! When we were deep into studies of philosophy at CUA and theology at WTU, with all the "isms" studied, he used to call me "Croninism." So I reciprocated and called him

"Hoganism." You can't get nicknames *from* just anybody! Can't give them *to* just anybody either!

IDIOSYNCRASIES

I've had my share of nicknames awarded me over the years, which I find amusing. They indelibly bond me with certain people, and certain times of my life when I remember them. They also help me to laugh at myself and my own idiosyncrasies and peculiarities . . . which I invite you to do as well, because they are many!

My name is Kevin Cronin. I've been called "Kevsy Love" by Barbara Brady in the fifth grade, at American Martyrs school in Bayside, Queens. My brother Gerard gave a title to me and our fantasy singing group in eighth-grade summering at Pine Grove, Connecticut: "Friar Kevsy and The Imperials."

Brother John Bosco, who could have modeled for that famous friar cookie jar, while working at our famous church in New York City on 31st Street, used to call me, because of my long hair and beard in the seventies: "the poorman's Jesus Christ Superstar." Marina Naranja, the dedicated cook for so many of us who went through Holy Name College, whom we regarded as "Brother Jacoba," used to call me in her native tongue: "el niño de Praga." The friars knew that meant "the Infant of Prague."

At my first priestly assignment at St. Anthony Shrine, Boston, I was considered somewhat of a radical troublemaker by some older friars who used to call me "the infant of *plague*! Friar Simon Iocca, another great nickname-giver, a man himself full of interesting idiosyncrasies, sometimes known as "Simon the Simple, Prince of Pistoia," used to call me "LBJ," short for "Little Baby Jesus." Can't tell you how many times I've been called the "hippie priest." Corinne McGowan, one of my dearest parishioners at St. Mary's, Pompton Lakes, New Jersey, used to call me "Brother Kevin of the joyful socks!" She often gave me the socks to go with the name, because she knew I'd wear them! My good friend Gert who came to Italy on pilgrimage with me calls me "Padre Kevino." I always translate it in Italian as "Cue Vino," "What Wine!"

INTERESTING COMMENTS

I worked at Junior Village one evening a week for the five years I was in D.C., and at this orphanage for mostly little black children, I remember more than once when little children with big brown shiny eyes would look up at me in my flowing robes, long hair, and beard, and ask: "Is your name Jesus? Are you from heaven?" I would always tell them I was happy I reminded them of Jesus, because "that's my job," but that: "No, I'm not Jesus, I'm his helper!"

I've also been the privileged receiver of some fascinating comments which I write down, because my weak ego needs to remember them sometimes. After preaching at a friars' church on Long Beach Island, New Jersey, I've more than once been told that I remind people of a "clean George Carlin." I've also been delighted to have been told another time or two on that same island after a Mass when the people clapped after my sermon, "Bishop Sheen is not dead!" Someone recently compared me to a "young friar Benedict Groeshel, CFR." Take your pick if you know me. Or have a good laugh if you don't.

WHOLE WORLD WOULD BE CATHOLIC!

One that I will take to my deathbed with me, and that I think of whenever I wonder if it's all worthwhile, was given me by a former parishioner who had moved down to Brick, New Jersey and was so surprised when she saw me giving a mission at her parish. Geraldine McGlynn said: "If they were all like you, the whole world would be Catholic!" The Irish have a lovely way with words! Cash that one up to the Blarney Stone!

THE FUNNIEST

Giving a mission at St. Frances de Chantel Parish at Wantagh, Long Island, a young mother came up to me after we celebrated the children's Mass. Her young special child of seven had told her that when he first saw me walking up the aisle for the entrance procession, that "Look ma, Jesus is here today!" But when I opened my mouth at the altar that he had changed his mind: "No, Ma, It's not Jesus. It's Robin Williams!" You gotta laugh!

friar Kevin

* * *

Who's Who Contest

Time to have a little fun! By the way, did you know this is an *interactive book*? It is, you know. Interactive stuff doesn't just happen on modern-day computers and discs. It happens in modern-day books. What do you think, we're still back in the Middle Ages? Get with it! No, it's not a disc to insert into your computer, but hopefully already this has been an interactive book inserting a little bit more of joy or hope into you.

Anyway, at this point of the book I want to check out to see how much you've been paying attention! Want to have a little fun and introduce you to a contest so that you can interact directly with the friars you've been accompanying in this manuscript. I want to tell you how you can get involved with our *Who's Who Contest!* Before I do that I want to get you warmed up with a little friar trivia test!

ORDER OF FAT MEN

Do you know what the three initials *ofm* stand for? These are the letters we friars put after our name when signing something or when being addressed formally. Some members of my own family don't know after twenty-six years! So, don't feel bad.

No, it's not the Order of Franciscan Monks. Friars were a new invention! Kind of a "remake" of a monk! We don't like being called monks even though we may look like one!

It's not Order of Franciscan Missionaries either, even though this wouldn't be too bad. Cause we do have a mission with lots of work to do! Just like every Christian does!

It's not Out For Money either! nor is it for the Order of Fat Men, though most fill out the robes very well, which, by the way are handmade by our professional tailor whose name happens to be Brother Juniper!

O.F.M. stands for the Order of Friars Minor! That's the name St. Francis gave his brothers, the order of lesser brothers, in other words. He always wanted his friars to be with the little people, the ordinary, not the "majors," or the powerful bigshots of the day! Down to earth, earthy! OK, that's settled!

You've heard about friar Kevin's nicknames in the past chapter, we want to see how carefully you've been reading. Can you figure out the nicknames of some of the other friars from the list below? If you're not in the mood for this, turn the page or come back when you wish. Below is a list of some names some of these friars may be called. Can you figure them out? Contest rules are in the appendix.

FRIAR NICKNAMES

Hans Van Anglican
Msgr. Dineen
Blue Eyes
The Cloud of Unknowing
Derf
Long Island Duckman
Chuck
The Beloved of God
Spaceman

Boody Wha
The Book of Kells
Sloppy Joe
Little Caesar
Red Sox Joe
Dooney
Wacko
Tush
Silver Fox

INTERACTIVE CONTEST

There is a listing of the complete names of the friars who have written in this book in the Appendix, with some facts about their lives which might help you figure out who's who and how to win the contest! Maybe this will cause you to pay more attention through the remainder of the work! What, do you think we're telling you all this stuff for our health? We want you to be a winner!

I hope you can say after reading this book: "I never met a friar that I didn't feel better after I did!" We hope you have met us! And we hope you are feeling somewhat better after a good dose of some "friar's brew" for your soul!

This section is just a bit of trickery and playfulness, a bit of good humor. We need much more of it. By the way, did you know that a new McDonald's is built somewhere every twenty-two hours? I don't know why I just said that! But I hope you got a chuckle out of it. God knows, we need more of it. You gotta laugh! It reminds us Who's Who, and Who's in charge.

friar Kevin

Racquetball

No one has ever accused me of being a gifted athlete. One of the few reasonably good attempts at becoming one came about fifteen years ago when I was stationed in Buffalo, New York. I took up racquetball. I had been a jogger for a while at the time and needed something to do for indoor exercise during the snowy winters which that city is famous for.

Another friar and I found a good rate at one of the local clubs and began playing. After about the third visit to the courts we met two other men who were also beginners. We got along and decided to continue learning the game and playing against one another. The following week after we had finished we were sitting in the sauna, relaxing, all of us but Frank. His friend told us that Frank almost didn't come to play that day, but had decided to do so at the last minute to take his mind off things. His wife had been killed that weekend in a car crash with a truck.

No sooner than we had been told this Frank entered the sauna room, clad, like the rest of us, only in a towel. We offered him our condolences. Frank did not yet know that we were friars. He cried a bit, then told us about the funeral Mass and that the thought entered his mind during the Mass that he really should get back to Church, but just didn't know what was entailed, or how to approach a priest. He was incredulous when we told him who we were. "God must really have a sense of humor having me meet up with two priests in the sauna at a racquetball court."

He came back to our friary with me that day and attended the noontime Mass, receiving Communion for the first time in a while. About a year later I married him to his second wife. We don't play racquetball any more. We're still friends and Frank continues to go to Church regularly. God indeed has a sense of humor!

As I look back on each of these stories I find that they truly are stories of joy, even the ones touched with sorrow, and that they are modern-day parables. As I meet with people in the places where I preach parish missions, and listen to their stories of faith, it seems that God is continually rewriting the Scriptures in the lives of his people. Perhaps those who read these stories will recognize their own story and the chapter, verse, or even the whole book of Scripture that the Lord is writing and telling in their own lives. I think that ministry for us friars lies exactly in this process. We don't have to bring something to people, or impart something, just tell our story so that others can more clearly tell theirs and all of us can continue to see that Jesus' story is ours too.

friar John A

* * *

Uh-Oh, God's Sending an Audit

Recently, someone excitedly said, "I see you're in the paper— the *Standard and Times*!" (that's Philly's diocesan paper). No way, no reporter has been here in a long while. The next day someone showed me the paper, "See, I told you so!" I looked. Hmmmmm . . . interesting idea.

Some reporter disguised himself as a homeless person and spent two weeks going around Philadelphia checking out the services for street people and the poor. No sweat. We're too far from the Center City. He never would come here. I just glanced quickly over the full page article. Uh-oh . . . I see "St. Francis Inn" once. Oh, there it is again . . . ooooh. My heart races a bit. Oh, there in another place . . . and again.

SWEATY PALMS

Oh God, when was that? What day? Was that the day we ran out of bread? Was that when we had to ask a guest to leave? My palms started to sweat. I started reading in detail. The man had come here *four* times. Oh, no! There's bound to be something. Was that the time Carlisle got under my skin? Was Sr. Mary having a "bad hair day"?

Deciding to face the music, I read on: "At St. Francis Inn the staff was very friendly." "They didn't rush you, and seemed genuinely happy to be of service." "When I asked the hour of the meal, a kind white-haired friar told me I'd never remember the schedule, so he went into the Inn and returned with a pen and paper to write it out for me." Whew! That was me! Thank God, I must have been good that day! (But did he *have* to mention the hair?)

GOOD FOOD

"The food was good and plenty of it." "The Inn is owned and run by Allegany Franciscan sisters." (Wait until our friar provincial hears that!) "When I inquired about shelter, a Franciscan sister patiently called several agencies for me. She was pleasant and thoughtful." (That was Sr. Mary. The reporter's beginning to lose credibility.)

OASIS OF PEACE! WE PASSED!

He liked the Inn so much that he returned three other times during his adventure and finally concluded that "St. Francis Inn in the Kensington Section of Philadelphia, is an oasis of peace in a sea of poverty and despair." Yeah! We passed! Thank you, Jesus!

Later the article appeared in the Brooklyn Diocese's *Tablet*. It was also the front page article complete with a picture of our Inn, in the Juneau Alaska Diocesan paper.

Boy, have I been nice to everyone lately! You never know who you are dealing with, just who may pop in. The author says in Hebrews 13:1–3: "Love your fellow Christians always. Do not neglect to show hospitality, for by that means some have entertained angels without knowing it." And of course in the Gospel of Matthew 25:35, 40 "I was a stranger and you welcomed me." And "As often as you did it for one of my least brothers and sisters, you did it for me."

friar Michael

* * *

Street Preaching Class

The fall of 1983 brought my second visit to Chicago, the first one having been little more than a "drive through" ten years earlier. I'd been ordained a priest about six months by then and assigned to a parish in New Jersey. I was already "stressed" by the responsibility of having to stand up in front of people and to preach so frequently, at least once every day easily. The chance to get away for a few days presented itself so I headed west to attend a national convention of liturgical artists. The program was quite good, but hectic. On the final evening I decided to "cut" the session so that I could walk around downtown Chicago.

After having walked around for several hours, up and down the Million Dollar Mile to the Water Works and all around the Loop, I started back to the friary where I was staying and noticed a good-sized crowd gathered on the sidewalk just a few hundred feet ahead of me.

CURIOSITY LED ME

Curiosity led me over to see a man in a business suit standing in front of a station wagon that had a short legged artist's easel set up on its roof. As the man spoke he painted on the canvas that was set up on the easel. At first I thought he might be a street artist who was explaining his latest work, but as I looked on the canvas I saw a hill and a dark sky and three crosses on the hill. As I moved into the crowd I heard the man speak and realized that he was a street preacher. It was after 11:00 P.M. and the crowd was made up of a group that were obviously no stranger to being out late on the streets of Chicago . . . tight short skirts on the ladies and lots of gold chains around the gentlemen's necks. Also, many obviously homeless people and immigrants. I was humbled by the scene.

HERE I WAS

Here I was a Franciscan and a newly ordained priest, and I was walking around the streets of Chicago as a tourist and here was this man preaching, and preaching to a group of people that I wouldn't have much time for. I felt a little sad but listened and watched on in hope that I might pick up a good idea to enliven my own preaching.

ARE YOU SAVED?

As he finished his painting and sermon, the crowd began to disperse and I turned to continue my walk home when someone tapped me on the shoulder and asked me the time, "11:35," I replied. Before the "five" came out I was hit with another question, "Do you know Jesus Christ?" And then, "Do you accept Jesus as your personal Savior?" The questions were coming from a well scrubbed all-American looking young man. He was rather nervous as he fired question after question not giving me any chance to reply, but usually offering his own answer by way of a verse of Scripture quoted chapter and verse. The questions and answers came fast. As I surveyed the street around us I noticed at least fifteen other young men and women engaging passerbys, tourists, and street people, in what appeared to be conversations like my own.

As he pelted me with questions, I realized this young man had no idea who I was. I waited nearly fifteen minutes but finally he either ran out of questions and answers or he'd worn himself out. In response to his early question I began to tell him how I knew Jesus Christ. The Jesus Christ that I knew was not abstract or "pie in the sky" but very real and made manifest by the loving people I'd been surrounded with all my life. As I spoke I began to feel myself getting more and more animated and speaking very freely with great conviction.

ADRENALIN WAS PUMPING

After a few minutes I realized that some of the other people who were either standing around or engaged in conversation like my own began to stand around me and were listening to me. This further encouraged me and I felt the adrenaline pumping through me. As I finished there were nearly thirty people standing around me applauding. The painter/preacher didn't get that.

In a moment of light conversation I learned the young man's name was Dan and that he was a student at a local Bible college. He was on the street that night because it was part of a street preaching course that he was taking. The other young people out there were also part of Dan's class. The instructor had left after he painted the picture leaving the class to experience street ministry firsthand.

The excitement of "turning the table" on that street preaching class and redeeming myself in light of my Franciscanism buoyed my confidence. I didn't have much trouble preaching after that night.

"Blessed is that servant of God who finds all his/her joy in the words and deeds of our Lord and uses them to help others love God gladly." St. Francis of Assisi.

friar Ron

* * *

I'll Dance with Jesus

Gerri sat in her wheelchair, a warm smile on her face and a rosary in her hands, as we arrived at her home to share the parish mission with her. This is one of the truly delightful parts of the missions we conduct with the Franciscan Ministry of the Word, bringing the love and prayers of the parish to its shut-ins, and letting parishioners know that they are included in the prayers of those confined to the home. As I prepared to share the Eucharist, with tears in her eyes she exclaimed, "My Jesus, how can I thank you? How can I thank you enough for all you've done for me?" After giving her Communion I told her what a gift it was for me to see faith like hers, how it strengthened my faith. She said:

> Faith is a gift, a precious gift Father, and I almost lost it. You see, I'm in this wheelchair because I was hit by a drunk driver when I was forty-two years old. I became angry and bitter and figured God had forgotten me. I told the priest not to bother coming by and I had all the religious articles removed from this house. I kept to myself and became miserable and grouchy. No one wanted to come near me, not even my family.
>
> After about ten miserable years I woke up one morning, looked at the wall above my bed, and saw the crucifix. At first I was upset. I didn't know how it got there and I was going to have my daughter take it down. All of a sudden I started to cry, I looked at Jesus on that cross and said to him, "Lord, other than these mangled legs of mine I'm a healthy woman. I'm probably going to be around this world for a while. I guess I'll have to learn how to be happy living in the wheelchair." A tremendous peace came over me and has grown in me ever since. I'm one of the happiest people in the world and its been ten years now and I know that my Jesus is always watching over me. He's everything for me.

Gerri had not been cured. She was still in her wheelchair, but she has certainly been healed by the Lord because her bitterness and anger was replaced by peace and happiness, his peace and happiness. So often I find that the real miracles in life happen in this way if only we have eyes to see. Real healing doesn't necessarily mean that our sicknesses and problems will go away. It means rather that we realize that God is with us in the situation, doing for us what we can't do for ourselves. It means placing ourselves in God's hands as we journey toward the kingdom where all sorrow, pain, and sadness will be taken away.

Gerri knew this instinctively, for before I left her she said, "I can't wait to meet Jesus *face to face*. I know that when I do, I'll get out of this wheelchair and dance with him."

friar John A

6

Complete Joy

All this I tell you that my joy may be yours,
and that your joy may be complete.
John 15:11

Help Me See!

Last October, I was driving from St. Bonaventure University down to Westchester County with three admissions counselors. We were on a mission, a recruiting trip to attract high school seniors to attend St. Bonaventure University. The trip would take a total of six to seven hours.

Half way through the trip, we stopped to get some gas. A few of us decided to get a little snack to hold us over through the rest of the trip. My snack of choice was something I can rarely resist: a Häagen Dazs dark chocolate/vanilla ice cream bar. As I delightfully savored the taste of the dark chocolate covering and the vanilla ice cream in my mouth, I noticed that a tiny piece of the chocolate fell onto my shirt. My shirt was a colorful dark blue rugby shirt with turquoise and lavender stripes across the chest and sleeves. There was also one slim white stripe which went through the design.

I searched my shirt for the tiny piece of chocolate which had fallen. I found it (of course) on the slim white stripe across the chest of my shirt. I hate when that happens! My unscientific calculations estimate that the chance of a tiny piece of chocolate falling onto that white stripe on my shirt was about one percent or less. Why couldn't it have fallen on the colorful part of my shirt, on my pants, or on the car seat or floor? I was unable to take the piece of chocolate off my shirt without a stain. It figures.

We arrived at the hotel just in time to get to our rooms, settle in, meet for dinner, and then get ready for the admissions program. I threw some water on my face, brushed my teeth, and then sat on the edge of the bed to catch some of the New England Patriots football game.

Then my eye caught sight of something on my pants. I looked down to find that a huge hunk of chocolate had fallen from the ice cream bar onto my pants in the area around the crotch. I couldn't believe how big it was, and how dried out and ground into my pants it had become in only four hours. Then I was remembering how we had walked in and out of the lobby a few times, first to check in, and then to bring our luggage into the hotel. It must have looked odd to say the least, a grown man walking around with a large hunk of dark chocolate ground into the lap of his tan colored pants. How intriguing! What a slob. Most of all, I couldn't believe that I hadn't seen the piece of chocolate fall or at least *noticed* it on my pants after it had fallen.

We were due to meet for dinner in the hotel restaurant in ten minutes. I hadn't bothered to pack another pair of pants because the trip only included two overnights, and I knew I would be wearing my Franciscan habit for the scheduled programs. I like to travel light. For some reason, the whole situation struck me as funny and I found myself laughing in my hotel room. I called one of the admissions counselors and fortunately for me, he had packed an extra pair of pants which fit me perfectly. I was spared the further embarrassment of walking around with a dark chocolate stain on the lap of my pants. We had a good laugh about the whole situation and I came away with a story to tell.

But I still wonder how often I pay more attention to the smaller annoying things in life, while completely missing (at least for a while) the bigger picture. I call this tunnel vision. It is the tendency to focus on the negative, the pain or struggles in our lives while paying less attention to the positive, the gifts and the good things. Tunnel vision, if it takes root in us, robs us of our joy and gratitude.

We miss the gifts that God gives to us every day. We lack appreciation for the beauty of creation, the warmth of the sun, a soft spring rain, a cool summer breeze, a thirst-quenching drink or a delicious meal. We take for granted the significant supportive relationships in our lives; family, friends, colleagues, our faith community or religious community. We fail to be touched by the supportive and loving presence of the Lord in our lives, the reality of the Spirit among us, which comforts us in our struggles and challenges us to grow.

Tunnel vision causes us to focus on what brings us down rather than what lifts us up. It brings death, not life. And it is our choice. We either reject tunnel vision as harmful to us and thereby choose life, or we unknowingly embrace it without realizing that we are hurting ourselves and by extension, those around us.

I am grateful that I was invited by a huge hunk of dark chocolate on the lap of my tan slacks to examine my own sense of vision. I commit myself once again to looking for the big picture rather than allowing myself to be preoccupied by the smaller, more negative or painful pieces. I believe that a more balanced outlook is essential in our efforts to reach our potential as human beings, following the Lord, and serving him in and through one another.

friar John K

* * *

Marriage Country Style

In the interior of Brazil, ranches can be several hours distant from the nearest town. The ordinary tenant farmer would not own a car. Weddings would be planned for a market day when the whole family and group of friends could hitch a ride on the back of a truck to come to the church.

The wedding, with all the preparations, would be accomplished in one day. A Brazilian couple from the country would come to town on the back of a truck, with all their relatives. They would go to the store to rent a wedding dress. Then they would get the required forms for a civil wedding, make their vows before the town magistrate, then come to the church, dressed in their wedding clothes, to fill out the forms, go to confession, and pronounce their vows in the church.

One couple had arrived at the front door. He in his dark suit and tie, which appeared to be strangling him, she in her rented dress and shoes.

They filled out the forms, and we proceeded to church, where as was the custom, they asked to go to confession before the marriage. I pointed to the confessional and went into the priest's side. As I opened the small sliding door I was amazed to see the couple kneeling side by side on the other side of the screen. They were relieved to discover that they did not have to make their confession together. After that was straightened out, the wedding went off without a hitch.

INVASION OF NORMANDY

Afterwards, the family and friends greeted them outside the church, and the truck came to take everybody home. It was a large open truck used for hauling grain. The cab would hold three people, the other twenty-five to thirty would crowd into the back. The happily married couple approached the truck, the groom and the best man climbed into the cab with the driver, the bride hitched up her long white gown, threw her leg over the tire, and swung up onto the back of the truck.

I like to ponder this memory as I watch young American suburban couples plan for a wedding that is more complex than the invasion of Normandy.

friar Charley

* * *

God's Book

Many friars don't even know this story! It's about how my first book got discovered—*Kenosis: Emptying Self and the Path of Christian Service*, also published by Continuum. Many people thought I paid for it to be, or bribed someone to publish it. I want to tell how it all happened. It's why I do call it "God's Book."

It was originally my master's thesis written for my M.A. in theology from the Washington Theological Union, where my area of concentration was pastoral field. I did my pastoral in depth experience at our church of St. Francis of Assisi in Midtown, New York City, right by Penn Station. My thesis was to be a critical self-evaluation integrating my knowledge of theology with the practice.

I took an original phenomenological approach choosing a particular theme through which to analyze myself and my ministerial experience: *kenosis*, a word that describes what Jesus did in becoming one of us in Paul's letter to the Philippians 2:5. That theme I felt was at the core of the mystery of Jesus, and therefore at the heart of every Christian, and certainly anyone would claim to serve and live the gospel in ministry.

I worked hard on it. I wanted to write it well. I wanted it to be a significant reflection integrating all I had learned in the thirteen years of preparation for priesthood. I thought that if it was done well, perhaps it just might be a model of ministerial reflection and Christian living for others. However, I only thought it would be published *posthumously*! Part of my requirement for my degree was to take an oral examination on my thesis. I was delighted that the board passed me "with distinction," which I never had heard of before.

ON THE SHELF
By the way, I recently saw it stated that the "shelf life" of the average American is 27,000 days! Anyway on my shelf the thesis went, till fifteen years later I was giving a sermon at St. Mary's in Pompton Lakes, New Jersey, where I was assigned from 1987 to 1993. I was waxing eloquent on the scripture "Unless the grain of wheat falls to the ground. . . Unless you lose your life . . . Whoever humbles themselves will be exalted. . . ." And I held up my newly dusted off manuscript, and said: "I should know something about this! I wrote my whole thesis on it." Didn't seem to impress anyone.

THE LITTLE LADY
Except one, a little ol' lady with kerchief on a tilted head, wielding a shopping bag, with cane in the other hand, says to me after the Eucharist: "OOO, can I read it?" I did not know her. Who was this woman? I said: "OK, but you better have it back by the next weekend! It's my only copy, and there's a long line waiting to read it."

She came back next weekend and said that she had taken a good nap to be fully rested, so she could concentrate and read my manuscript at fifty-page intervals. Well, she said: "I couldn't put it down. You should publish it! I've read it already three times!" Who is this lady? I said "Sure, I'm a busy parish priest. I have no time for that kind of project." I had already done enough work on that 150-page manuscript the first time. That was that!

IN LOVE'S RADIANCE

Later that summer I learned that my new interesting friend's name was Naomi Gilpatrick. She sometimes summered in Rockport, Massachusetts, where she spent some time growing up, and also caring for her elderly, infirm, and dearest mother.

One day she almost got killed at the city dump by a backhoe, whose driver did not see her car at the recycling site. Nearly killed, but thank God, only frightened, but the huge tractor tore off her car door on the driver's side. So her car got laid up. She was left to doing her errands on foot.

One day she wanders past an old brick building on Main Street which she remembered was the former home of an old friend. "Hum, let me go in and see what's happened to it," says Naomi. It turns out to be a book publisher and store for Amity, a Catholic publisher. They found her to be an interesting character as I did, made some conversation, gave her a book, and told her to drop in anytime.

Naomi with a hop, skip, and a jump made her way home, cane in hand, and thought she would take a look at the book the man gave her. It was *In Love's Radiance*, by Linda Sabbath. Well, the word kenosis came up. She had never seen it before my manuscript. "I better tell Mr. Payne about Fr. Kevin's work."

CAN I READ IT?

He later called me telling me how he had met my interesting friend who told him with great detail and enthusiasm that she "knew a priest who wrote a *whole book* about kenosis"! He asked me: "Can I read it?" I cracked up! I said: "I'd be glad if *anyone* read it! It has been on my shelf for fifteen years." I hung up.

Now who is this guy? And what is Naomi up to now? I didn't do anything. I was busy being a parish priest.

Five days go by, Mr. Payne calls again: "Did you send the manuscript yet? I'm waiting for it!" I loved when he called it a "manuscript"! No, I didn't but I sent it as soon as I could. This was early September 1989. I didn't hear from him for the rest of the month, I figured that was the end of that . . . until the feast of St. Francis, October 4.

When I returned from a neighboring friary celebration, I checked my phone messages. My heart jumped! One pink slip said: "Happy Feast of St. Francis! I have good news for you about your book!" I love when he called it a "book." I called Richard Payne back.

He said: "I feel the same way as Naomi does; I would like to publish your work! Can I send you the contracts?" I could not contain myself. I was laughing my rear end off! I told him, "Of course, be my guest!" He told me this is how he often finds his best works. They seem to find him. I thanked him, and had a happy feast of St. Francis, the master of kenosis.

WHO WERE THEY?

I only found out later that Richard Payne used to work for a well-known Catholic Publisher, Paulist Press, and that he was editor-in-chief of their Classics in Western Spirituality series, editing works on Francis and Claire, Bonaventure, and other spiritual heavyweights. When I found out that *he* found my work valuable, it was a real thrill, to say the least. He sold his company to Element, an English company that was the publisher for the first printing of *Kenosis*. He later left that company because of their involvement with the "New Age" and the occult, and of their downplaying of Christian authors. He was an angel at the right place and time to have the book finally published for my eleventh birthday bash and family reunion at St. Mary's, February 29, 1992.

My little ol' lady, was *Dr.* Naomi Gilpatrick, a freelance writer, poet and book reviewer herself! Not to mention that she was a professor in language arts at Seton Hall University and William Paterson College, with her other credentials: BA, summa cum laude, from College of St. Elizabeth; MA, Phi Beta

Kappa, University of Michigan; EdD, Teachers College, Columbia University. Wow! My little lady was Dr. Gilpatrick! God knows how to pick and send angels my way! Naomi has become a dear friend, spiritual confidant, and anchorite. Her gentle piety and dynamic wisdom qualify her also as my agent. She recently told me that Frank Baum the author of the *Wizard of Oz* sent his book to fifty-four publishers before it was ever accepted! I never had to send it anywhere!

Because of all this I called *Kenosis* God's book! God inspired it! God got it off my shelf after fifteen years! God got it published with a little help from some of his good friends! It is in its second printing with Continuum. To God alone be all the glory, now and forever, and ever and ever! Amen.

friar Kevin

* * *

Step by Step

My father passed away in November 1990 after a fifteen-month battle with cancer. The time of his illness and the months following his death were extremely difficult ones for me. I experienced the personal pain of grief during those times, as well as the anger that is typically associated with grief. I was also hurt by a lack of support in some instances where I expected a more compassionate response.

My struggle was compounded by the fact that I was experiencing a dry period in my life spiritually. My relationship with the Lord suffered greatly in the midst of this painful period. I felt betrayed by the Lord and angry at him. I avoided spending time in personal prayer because I didn't want to sit alone with him in quiet stillness and face everything that was happening within me and between us. In short, I put my relationship with the Lord on the shelf.

Six months after my father's death, I finally took something that I desperately needed. I began a week-long silent retreat at Bethlehem Hermitages in Chester, New Jersey. It was time to face who and what I had been avoiding. I unpacked my belongings in the hermitage and walked down the hill, then up the stairs to the chapel. The experience that followed was truly beautiful. I captured it in verse later that day so I would always have it to remember.

BEHIND THE CHAPEL DOOR

Step by step and all alone, the chapel stairs I slowly climb,
With nervous fear and repressed tears, I realize now's the time.
You've called me up these stairs, my Lord, I felt you call my
    name,
No turning back, I know I must confront this fear and pain.

Near the top, I stretch my hand out reaching for the door,
My tension, fear and apprehension intensify some more.
I open up the chapel door and gingerly walk through,
I close the chapel door and stand there face to face with you.

Tentatively, curiously, I scan this sacred space,
Its beauty and simplicity reflect your warmth and grace.
I quietly step forward and with reverence gently bow,
I must renew our friendship, Lord, no better time than now.

I choose a space to sit with you, I want to start to pray,
I fear I'm at a loss for words, I don't know what to say.
Suddenly tears spring forth, I willingly let them go,
As the Spirit speaks and months of fragile feelings freely flow.

The Lord has touched my wounded heart and opened wide my
    feelings,
A cleansing bath, the flood of tears evokes in me a healing.
Release! Relief! Re-Naissance! My heart begins to soar,
As our friendship springs to life again behind the chapel door.

friar John K.

* * *

Louie the Pigeon

When I was a young boy growing up on Long Island, I like to think that I wasn't much different from a lot of kids my age in fifth and sixth grade. On a beautiful spring day, I couldn't wait for the school bell to ring in the afternoon. It wasn't just that I longed to play basketball, ride my bike, or go into the tree house that my brother and I built. I really looked forward to being with some forty-some odd homing pigeons that my brother and I had raised. It would take too long to explain how the two of us got involved in this hobby of ours. Suffice it to say that a lot of the neighbors were not too thrilled about the whole idea.

MY GRANDFATHER

One of those neighbors happened to be my Italian grandfather who lived next door. More than a few times he used to ask in his Italian accent: "Tommy, I wanna know ah, why ah, the piga, hava to landa onna my roof?" At his wits' end somedays, he'd say: "You know one of these ah daysa I'm a gonna taka my gunna and I'm gonna shoot!" Of course he never shot any of our fine feathered friends. But his roof was green, so you can figure it out yourself!

SETTING THEM FREE

This I can tell you. I always wanted to get home before my brother, because that left me with the wonderful task of unlocking the door of the pigeon coop, setting those birds free, letting them do what they do best. Fly! Maybe this will sound a little crazy to some of you, but when those birds would fly from the coop, I always had a sort of feeling that they were communicating to me.

As they flew from that coop one of the things that always caught my attention was the way they smacked their wings together. Of course the pigeons were only stretching their wings, but all those birds flapping their wings at the same time made sort of a clapping sound. And so in my kid imagination I pretended these pigeons were applauding for me for setting them free.

MY KID IMAGINATION

Then the pigeons would fly so high into the mighty blue yonder that they appeared to be no more than a dot in the sky. And in my kid imagination, I thought those birds were saluting the sun, the moon, and the clouds. And finally the pigeons would come back to the coop, but often in a swaying, gliding type of motion. And in my kid imagination I used to think that the birds were putting on a little dance for me.

You know, I have no scientific evidence that those pigeons were communicating with me or not, but I do believe this. I believe that every time we reflect on the death and resurrection of Jesus, and on such parables as the prodigal son, that our good God is communicating to us. He is saying: "I want to unlock the door of your heart. I want to set you free. I want you to do what you do best . . . to live and love in the freedom of God."

THE POPE SINS

And so in this little article what I'd like to bring up is not: "Gee, why do we sin?" Because everybody sins. The pope sins. Mother Teresa sins. That is a given. Perhaps Bishop Sheen said it best when he walked into a maximum security prison. In his opening remarks to the inmates, he said: "The only difference between you and me is that you got caught!" Now there was a man who was in touch with his humanness, and his capacity to sin. Maybe you heard the words of the late Cardinal Cushing of Boston who was asked: "When does a man stop having impure thoughts?" The cardinal is supposed to have responded: "Don't ask me! I'm only 78!" so we all sin. But why do we, like the pigeons in the coop, like the pigs in the pigpen, why do we stay in that dark smelly place we call sin? It is so obvious that Jesus wants to set us free.

IF THEY ONLY KNEW

I'm not sure if I have the answer to that question. But some years ago I remember watching a talk show on TV where the host asked a famous actress if she was concerned about anything. After all she seemed to have everything going for her. But she thought for a moment, saying rather soberly: "Yes, I'm afraid that if people really knew me the way I know me, I wonder if they would really like me?" I've never forgotten that answer. We all wonder about that, don't we?

Don't we all wonder: "If they really knew me. I mean really knew me the way I know me, would they really like me?"

And yet if there is one group of people on planet earth who should be able to say like St. Francis: "I am what I am before the Lord. Nothing else, nothing more, nothing less," it should be Catholics. We Catholics even make a sacred space and time we call the sacrament of confession/reconciliation to live out that deep truth in love. Unfortunately this is not always the Catholic experience.

It's not just that yellow journalism, cheap talk shows exist to make millions at the expense of people's foibles, and to destroy reputations. But a culture seems to have been created where the thought of unconditional love seems impossible to mediate. Be it a mom or dad, husband or wife, sister or brother, a teacher, or friend . . . people don't trust! And when someone tells you they had a bad experience in confession back when they were a kid or young adult, that doesn't help either. Still, the truth remains, the truth remains the truth, that when the father in the story of the prodigal son runs out to his son "full of compassion," so our God comes and has that full compassion towards us.

LOUIE STUCK ON THE GWB

You know, as my brother and I raised more and more pigeons, we were fascinated by those birds. In fact if you ever find some free time, it might be good to get yourself a book about pigeons.

Did you know, for example, that they have documented cases of pigeons who have crossed the Atlantic Ocean? Did you also know that they have dissected every part of a pigeon and they cannot figure out how these birds make it such distances?

My brother Dennis and I could never afford the pedigree birds, but we had a few that we knew were very smart. One of those birds we named Louie! He was an old bird, but we knew, a very smart one. We took him out to eastern Long Island once to test him out. We set him free about sixty miles from our house.

According to their manual Louie should have been back to the coop before we returned home that evening from the beach. Lo and behold he was there! We were so excited, we decided sometime later to have our dad set Louie free from somewhere in New Jersey. According to the manual, Louie should have made it back within two days. It took him a week. But we were still very excited, thrilled that he actually made it back at all! I remember asking my dad what he thought might have kept

Louie away for so long. No real lover of pigeons, dad responded with typical good humor, that "Louie probably got stuck on the George Washington Bridge!" (New York joke)

THE WAY HOME: LOUIE AND THE PRODIGAL SON

Finally we knew a neighbor who was going to Dayton, Ohio! This required lots of thought for my brother and me. Louie was not getting any younger! If we were to do it, we better do it quick. So, we did. According to the manual, Louie should have made it back in a week. We weren't that optimistic, but the fact that Louie had a mate sitting on eggs, would at least speed things along a little. Well, we waited one week; one week turned into two; and two weeks into two months. Before one knew it, spring turned into summer, summer into fall.

Lo and behold, one day I came home from school and sitting on the windowsill was Louie. To this day, at forty-seven years of age, I am still amazed about this pigeon! You'd think I would "get a life" but I do wonder how did this bird do it?

AN ENTIRE FLOCK OF PIGEONS

Amazing as this may be, I've heard other stories that I find even more captivating. In his book *The Kingdom of the Lonely God,* Fr. Robert Griffin tells the story of a man who sold his entire flock of pigeons to a bird fancier who lived on the other side of town. Now when the new owner got home with his new pigeons he did what pigeon people often do. He clipped the wings of the birds so that they would not fly back to the original owner. Well, one day the original owner was sitting in the back yard and lo and behold walking up the driveway on bloody, sore, tired feet was the entire flock of pigeons! My friends, I don't understand how these pigeons do it, and I don't know why we at times in our life's journey, because of sin, often feel so separated, alienated, and lost.

What I do know is this. The way home, which we all seek, is always possible. Along the way, our spirits, like those pigeons' feet, may grow bloody, sore, and tired, but the way home is always possible! And when we get there, isn't it true, when we have been welcomed, when we've been forgiven, don't we figuratively speaking, want to clap our hands? Don't we feel that our hearts want to soar? Don't we feel that we want to dance in the Spirit? Why? Because we have been set free once again, to do what we do best . . . to live and love in the freedom of the children of God.

FIVE MINUTES OLD

Sometimes when I look in the mirror, I too have those thoughts: "If people really knew me the way I know me, I wonder if they would really like me?" I don't think we can *live* that way! I believe what God is saying to us in Jesus and in the sacred Scriptures is: "I do know you the way you know you. I know you *better* than you know you! And I love you with an everlasting love!"

Some time ago I came across an article about G. K. Chesterton, the famous Catholic author, and Bernard Shaw, who were not only literary giants, but also good friends. One of the things Shaw could never figure out is why Chesterton became a Catholic.

In a letter to Chesterton, Shaw wrote in good humor: "I find the spectacle of your portly kneeling figure in the confessional to be incredible, monstrous, and comic!" This is what Chesterton wrote in response: "Well, when a Catholic comes from confession, he/she does truly by definition, step out into that dawn of their own beginning. In that dim corner, and in that brief ritual, God has really remade that person in God's own image. He may be grey and gouty; but he is only five minutes old!"

The faith of Catholics is often celebrated in and through sacraments. In the wonderful sacrament of reconciliation we do in faith step out into the dawn of our own beginning, where we have been remade in the "image and likeness of God," and where we once again have that feeling that we are only five minutes old.

And it is then and only then that we know the experience of Louie and the prodigal son. For it is then that we know where we really belong and to whom. It is then that we know that we are truly welcome once again, for we are *Home*! *Home* with the great God who gave us the freedom to leave and to fly in the first place! The door is always open! The key is under the mat! Welcome home! Come on in! Come home where you belong!

friar Thomas

Healing Touch

During the summer of 1981 I was working at Memorial Sloan–Kettering Cancer Center in New York City, as a per diem nurse. Sloan Kettering is a hospital for the treatment of patients who have cancer.

One of the patients I cared for that summer was Michael. Michael was then twenty-five years old with a diagnosis of leukemia. When I first met Michael he was up and about, filled with energy and hopeful that his cancer would go into remission. As the weeks and months of that summer progressed, he underwent intense chemotherapy. Because of the side effects of the therapy and the progression of his leukemia, Michael's condition deteriorated. He lost his appetite, he lost weight, his hair fell out, and he was confined to bed. Michael's prognosis went from hopeful to guarded.

Because of being confined to bed his body underwent changes that are associated with a person who is in bed for long periods. Among the many changes that occur, one is that the skin dries out, and the area of the body that dries out the most are the soles of the feet. Actually they can become very scaly. The nursing intervention is very simple; apply some lotion or oil in order to replace the moisture in the skin.

Michael's feet had become very dry and scaly, so for several days I was putting extra lotion on his feet several times a day hoping to reverse the extreme dryness. After the third day of doing this, he said to me, "Francis has anyone ever rubbed your feet?" "No," I said. "It feels so good," he replied. "I know they give me morphine to take away the pain I have, but when you rub my feet, it seems as if all the pain disappears. Also I know that I get tranquilizers to take away the anxiety I sometimes have, yet when you or my mom massage my feet, it is like all my anxiety dissolves."

Listening to what Michael said, I was happy that in some small way I was able to help him and ease his discomfort. I continued to put the lotion on Michael's feet and do whatever nursing interventions would help him in his care. As the summer months passed into early September, Michael's condition became critical, and by mid-September his body had succumbed to the cancer. He died just shy of his twenty-sixth birthday.

Michael taught me many things that summer, among them was the power of the human touch and how healing it can be on many levels. Little did I know how healing a foot massage could be, and especially for someone so ill. Only later did I learn that when we touch someone lovingly, such as holding a hand, or a loving embrace other physiological changes occur. A person's blood pressure drops, hemoglobin increases, healing hormones are released in the body, and in premature infants their birth weight increases considerably when they are held and stroked. For children who are hyperactive, simply holding their hand and rubbing it will often quiet them.

Caring for Michael that summer taught me a wonderful lesson, that we all have the gift of healing within us; it is as simple, and as powerful, as lovingly touching another.

friar Francis

* * *

Ol' Blue Eyes

One of the best features of preaching a retreat to people who have never laid eyes on you is that they have not yet heard your jokes and stories. Such was my advantage when I arrived in upstate New York recently to conduct a six-day retreat for Franciscan Sisters.

The Spirit was upon me and was being poured lavishly upon all the people present. I could sense that this was going to be a special, memorable retreat. The very old and the very young found themselves caught up in the loving, healing, forgiving spirit of God. In the midst of all this presence of the Spirit, I managed to insinuate some good gentle humor producing a few hearty laughs. The Spirit's humor, however, stole the show!

Midway through the week we celebrated the Mass of the Anointing of the Sick. After the homily, we bless the oils and I began anointing the Sisters. I experienced nothing special during the anointing except the joy that comes from looking into the eyes of each person and "communicating" with them as I spoke the words of comfort, healing, forgiveness, and touched their foreheads and the palms of their hands with the precious, sacred oil.

One week later I received a long letter from one of the Sisters who participated in the anointing. She wrote that she had been depressed and distracted, and had not wanted to come to the retreat. In May she was honored as teacher of the year in her diocese and was thrilled to receive such affirmation. By July, however, she developed a mysterious throat ailment that reduced her speaking (and teaching) capacity to a whisper. Was this some mean joke by God, she thought. She was angry at life, at her doctors, herself and God.

How could she spend a week in prayer and listen daily to some smiling Franciscan elaborate upon the goodness and kindness of God? She decided to come because she did not want to reveal her personal reasons to her minister general if she decided not to come to the annual community retreat. Besides, she did not want rumors to start about how serious her condition might be. She decided that the best and easiest thing to do is to show up. (Woody Allen was right when he said that 80 percent of life is just showing up.)

Coming now to the Anointing Mass, she debated whether or not she was an apt candidate for the Sacrament. When push came to shove, she came forward to be anointed. As she stood up to move to the center aisle, she suddenly experienced heat and warmth throughout her body. It startled her, yet she knew that she had to keep walking down the aisle for the anointing. Now, came the strange yet beautiful part. In her letter she described my face as radiant and my eyes the shiniest and bluest she had ever seen. A little bit of heaven came through the blue in those eyes, for she was touched by God at that moment and her throat condition disappeared. Praise the Lord!

A month later we arranged a meeting, and she was again struck speechless when she looked into my sometimes brown and sometimes green but never blue hazel eyes! I heard the Spirit sing—I Did It My Way!

friar Daniel

* * *

The Best Ride Home

When I was a young student friar I was asked to substitute teach a theology class for a friar who was sick at Archbishop Dennis J. O'Connell High School in Arlington, Virginia. It was Ash Wednesday. I'll never forget it. Because all twenty-five hundred students were packed into an auditorium for a compulsory school Mass for the beginning of Lent. I'll never forget that Mass. Kids were reading textbooks, talking to each other, fooling around. Things weren't that much better up on the stage (altar), where the priest looked bored stiff, along with everybody else up there. I said to myself, "If Jesus Christ came to this Mass, I don't think he would have even stayed." I know I didn't want to. What a drag!

For four great years I was part of our young friar retreat team that gave weekend retreats to high school students. It was a challenge! But it was usually fun! We were only five or six years older than some of them.

My classmate, friar Bob Hudak, old friend from when we were both freshmen in the high school seminary, and Dan Kenna had an idea. Two weeks before school started in September, they wanted to know if I wanted to teach at O'Connell with them? We want to be there on Monday morning with the kids after their great weekend retreats, to help them with their "fourth day." We would be giving all the retreats to all the seniors at DJO that year! Bob knew how to get me to do things! So I did in blind faith!

THE JOCK RETREAT

After the first two retreats which went well, there was the "jock retreat!" All the football team and all the track, and tough guys who could care less were making it! The girls all said to us: "Good luck brothers, with these guys! We'll be praying for you!"

What breakthroughs! What a weekend! Those guys shared, cried, sang all our great songs. What an experience! When we got back on Monday morning, senior boys could be heard singing through the hallways in conga lines, "O! O! O! How good is the Lord! I never will forget what he has done for me!" "Praise God! Praise God! Praise God in the morning, Praise God in the evening!" There was no stopping them!

They hated class Masses. They requested the principal to let them have one that Monday afternoon, so they could thank their classmates for all their love through their notes to them and their prayers.

A TWO-HOUR MASS

The following Wednesday was, you got it, Ash Wednesday! Five guys went up to Fr. McMurtrie, the principal, to ask if they could give the sermon to the whole school! Mike Nichols, the tough quarterback, was leading them! The Mass took two hours! The sign of peace was a half hour! Kids even went up on the stage to hug the priests! Nobody could believe their eyes!

What God had done! And what can happen in just one short year! Still to this day this was one of the most awesome experiences of God's power and the operation of the Holy Spirit that I have ever seen! These kids were changed! They experienced God's love and they actually looked like they were redeemed and happy to be Catholics!

This is one of the peak experiences of my life as a friar. Two men joined the friars from that class. You can ask any other friars there that day: Dan Kenna, Bob Hudak, Vince Licursi, Gary Kolarcik. Our car practically flew past the White House. We were so high on the Lord. It was the best ride home ever!

friar Kevin

* * *

A Cold Winter Day

I had just finished celebrating Mass at St. Francis Church on 31st Street in New York and was walking down the side aisle when I was greeted by Mary, a woman in her late sixties. She welcomed me to the church. It was the fall of 1974. I was newly arrived and swimming in a sea of new faces to meet. I greatly appreciated her warmth and hospitality. I had seen her before in the brief time since I had arrived in New York. She volunteered her services in different ways, including the breadline for the poor that the friars run at 31st Street. I thanked her for the welcome and told her that I could see that she was one of the "pillars" of the place. She smiled and told me how that came to be.

It was a cold winter day during the Depression. She had come into the church just to get off the street and get warm. "I had no desire to pray or go to Mass," she told me, "just to get warm."

One of our Franciscan brothers was cleaning one of the altar shrines and she offered to help. They spent about four hours changing altar cloths, scraping wax, and changing candles. When they were finished, he thanked her and said, "You're a kind and generous woman." "Kind and generous woman," she said. "You're really laying it on thick, brother. I'm no kind and generous woman. You don't even know who I am. I didn't even come here to pray. I just wanted to get off the street and get warm. Do you know who I am? I'm a prostitute, that's who I really am, for your information."

The friar was not at all flustered or taken aback by this she told me. He simply looked back at her and said, "You're the one who doesn't know who you really are. Who you are before God is the kind and generous woman who just helped me. That's who you really are."

"I left in a huff," Mary told me. "How dare he say that?— You don't know who you are." But those words haunted her, as she explained. She kept hearing them in her mind. Finally, about five weeks later she returned to St. Francis church. She slipped into one of the confessionals, made her peace with God, and completely turned her life around. She had discovered and embraced who she really was, a loving and generous person who was herself loved and cared for by a gracious and compassionate God.

I will never forget Mary. Her story will always remind me not only of God's love and goodness, but of the wonderful tradition of compassion and understanding that has been handed on to us friars today by those who have gone before us.

friar John A

* * *

What's So Great about That?

That question holds a lot more than you might think. In this world what do *you* think is really great? Why not stop reading this article and get a pen and paper, and list the things in this world you think are really great.

Being able to sing in front of an eighty-piece orchestra and lift the spirits of a stadium full of fans? Setting a new world record at the Olympics? Holding a political office? Being famous? Winning the lottery? What things do you really get excited about? Where do you put your energy and time? What are you talking about when you get animated?

I used to think that all those examples above would be truly great moments in life until one day I realized how God sees things. He tells us in Scripture, but I never really paid much attention to it until recently.

I was walking in downtown Boston. It was in October and I was returning to my friary in East Boston when, as a short cut to the subway, I walked through Jordan Marsh department store. I was immediately hit with the heavy smell of perfume that seems always to be in department stores' first floor, main door. Half-daydreaming, I walked by several signs that exclaimed in big bold free-style letters, SOPHIA! SOPHIA! SOPHIA! What brought me back to full consciousness was a huge picture of none other than Sophia Loren herself next to yet another "SOPHIA" scrawl. Then the explanation. "SOPHIA LOREN in person, Tuesday, October 7, two P.M. Second Floor. Introducing her new fragrance!"

I thought, "Wow, that's special! Sophia Loren coming to Boston? We're getting up in the world!" I was about ten feet past the picture when I thought, "Gosh, today is Tuesday, October 7!" I looked at my watch. "I can't believe it—1:50 P.M." I thought to myself, "You mean to tell me in ten minutes, the real Sophia Loren is going to be up that escalator on the second floor?" "Wow! This I gotta see. Wait till I tell the other friars at supper that I actually saw Sophia Loren. This will be great!"

I hurried to the escalator. When I arrived on the second floor, I was amazed. They had pushed all the counters aside and this big space was filled with more than a thousand people eagerly awaiting her arrival. It was a mob scene. People were standing shoulder to shoulder. There were reporters, lights, TV cameras, and a line of ladies each holding a large shopping bag emblazoned with the now familiar "Sophia" trademark.

They were lining up to have her autograph their purchases. This was great! I elbowed my way back against the wall, and waited, enjoying the whole scene. Then it happened. At five minutes after two, there was a flurry of activity in the corner of the room. The lights came on, the noise level increased, and a wedge of security men arm in arm cut through the crowd. First came the business executives with their suitcoats and ties and then . . . *her*!

She absolutely electrified the room as she entered! She stood head and shoulders above all those around her. All eyes focused on her. As one, the crowd pressed forward and began clapping and shouting. She is actually more beautiful in person than in her movies. The auburn hair, the high cheekbones, and the famous almond eyes! (Now don't get nervous here, we are just admiring God's beauty in his creatures.) Flashbulbs popped, cameras whirred, people shouted after her. Talk about an entrance! It was incredible! She moved to the table at the center of the room and started writing, smiling all the while. The chaos and excitement never let up. I could hardly wait to tell the other friars. This was great! After about twenty minutes of this I needed to continue on my way, so I reluctantly left the presence of this international star.

As planned, that night I regaled my community with every little detail of the Sophia Loren experience.

MICHELINA LAMONICA

The next morning I was in the lower church preparing for the daily Mass. The gospel was the story of the ambitious sons of Zebedee whose mother asked Jesus that her two sons sit, one at the left and one at the right of Jesus when he came into his kingdom. My mind was racing to get some thoughts together on that gospel incident when in the sacristy came a little old withered Italian lady, Michelina LaMonica. She has been a parishioner of the church since before Abraham. Her tiny stooped frame holds a face with a mass of wrinkles and an almost sorrowful expression. "Father," she said, "Could you open the door to the upstairs church?" "Sure, Michelina, but what are you going to do up there?" I asked. "I'm going to dust the pews." "You are? Why? Who asked you to do that?" "Oh, no one," she replied. "I do it every week so the ladies won't get their coats dirty when they come to church on Sunday." "Gosh, that's nice, Michelina. There, the door is open."

Then I returned to the sacristy and went back to my gospel passage. "Then Jesus called his disciples together and said, "If you really want to be great. . . . Then you must serve the rest." "Now let me see," I pondered to myself, "what can I say about this thought . . . greatness . . . service . . . ?

And then, *pow!* It hit me! Right in front of my eyes. I saw the vivid image of two women! Sophia Loren and Michelina LaMonica! Where does greatness lie according to Jesus' definition? Yesterday afternoon—that I thought was so great. Did anything at all happen that was really great? Not one thing was great about it! The reporters were there to get their story. The TV cameras were there to get a segment on the evening news. The business executives were there to make money. Sophia was there for fame and money. And I, the holy friar, was there so I could brag to my friar brothers that I had seen a movie star!

GREATNESS

Not one great thing happened that could even remotely be called great. None of us were there for others . . . we were all in it for ourselves. And then there was tiny, frail Michelina LaMonica standing there with her tote bag full of dust rags intent on seeing that the ladies keep their coats clean. It is almost laughable to compare these two women according to any of this world's standards: fame, beauty, money, power, or talent. There would be no contest. But when we use Jesus' criterion of greatness—service—then we begin to see what's truly important. We are given a hint of God's criteria in Matthew 25, "When I was hungry . . . you gave me . . . When I was thirsty you gave me . . . you visited me . . . you comforted me . . . .

Now, try looking at the world through the eyes of Jesus. Use His standard, not our own. What's great now? Go back to the list you made at the beginning of this chapter. Now ask yourself. "What's so great about that?" Think of Sophia and Michelina and you just might never look at the world the same again, I know I don't.

friar Michael

Conclusion

Playfulness

As I look back over what has been written by the friars in this book, a mosaic appears . . . a mosaic of what a modern-day friar is really like; a collage colored by mystical, almost magical moments in their lives which invite the reader to go "behind the veil" with them. Yes, the reader has been invited to enter into those privileged moments, those profoundly mysterious and almost magical moments when a friar minor either was a witness to, or himself had, the deepest of divine encounters.

ESCORTS

Yes, the reader has been escorted sometimes to the heights of Mt. Sinai with these simple, humble men of God, these lesser brothers. When an unexpected sniffle was caught or a gentle smile wrought, the reader had been disarmed, has had to "take off their shoes" once again, because they had found themselves indeed on "holy ground," perhaps standing before an unexpected bush that was burning in the pages of this manuscript.

DIVINE PRESENCE

Yes, the reader has been on pilgrimage to the sanctuary of the Temple in Jerusalem, accompanied by one of its friar-priests pointing them towards the new and heavenly Jerusalem. They have drawn near with joy to the divine presence, have approached cautiously to the curtain in the Temple behind which dwells the "holy of holies." At times the pilgrim had delighted in what the guide reported would soon be disclosed, and was even teased by the upbuilding of its utter simplicity and evangelical clarity.

At times the pilgrim with courage—and all pilgrims need courage—has gone through the veil with these men "with sandals on their feet, who celebrate Passover as if on pilgrimage" (Exodus 12:11), and has experienced with them the very same divine meeting, the divine presence, the experience of the holy . . . the divine encounter in the unexpected ordinary, or in a very mysterious depth of an extraordinary human experience.

SPIRIT AT PLAY

Once again the Spirit of God and the incarnate Word, Jesus Christ, have been at play once again during the reader's quiet sigh or gentle chuckle at the divine mystery at play. Please pass the Chiclets!

SPIRITUAL SOUNDBITES

No one story, no one friar could encapsule the entire mystery for the reader. So the collage has been presented to invite an experience in varied and marvelous ways with lighthearted spiritual soundbites and in the seemingly superficial, as well as in the rare and profound and definitely awesome.

COLORFUL COLLAGE

The mosaic creates a picture of what the modern-day follower of the little poor, yet joyful man of Assisi looks like. And it needs to be seen all together. The very nature of brotherhood and community is that only together will we radiate the face of the glorious Christ of the beloved Francis. And in his own words from *Mirror of Perfection*, Francis describes what makes him joyful, what the perfect friar would be like:

> The most blessed father, having in some degree transformed the friars into saints by the ardor of his love and by the fervent zeal for their perfection which fired him, often pondered on the virtues that ought to adorn the good friar minor. He used to say that a good friar minor should imitate the lives and possess the merits of these holy friars: the perfect faith and love of Brother Bernard; the simplicity and purity of Brother Leo, who was a man of most holy purity; the courtesy of Brother Angelo,

who was the first nobleman to enter the order, and was
endowed with courtesy and kindness; the gracious look
and natural good sense of Brother Masseo, together with
his noble and devout eloquence; the mind upraised to
God, possessed in the highest perfection by Brother Giles;
the virtuous and constant prayers of Brother Rufino, who
prayed without ceasing, and whose mind was fixed ever
on God, whether sleeping or working; the patience of
Brother Juniper, who attained the state of perfect patience because he kept the truth of his low estate con-
stantly in mind whose supreme desire was to follow Christ
on the way of the cross; the bodily and spiritual courage
of Brother John of Lauds, who in his time had been
physically stronger than all men; the charity of Brother
Roger, whose life and conversation was inspired by fervent charity; the caution of Brother Lucidus, who was
unwilling to remain in any place longer than a month,
for when he began to like a place, he would at once leave
it, saying, "Our home is not here but in heaven."

The last comment about Lucidus would make most friars
chuckle, because it could be said about many friars who like to
keep on the move and "in the air" a lot of the time! *No* one
had the whole thing! But together they would make up the
perfect friar; and *together* we would most perfectly radiate the
risen Christ and show forth the image of God!

MODERN MINSTRELS
Yes, the divine at play, the divine revealing itself through those
first twelve of Francis, and now through these modern-day minstrels for the holy. Troubadour tour guides at the end of the
twentieth century.

The playful image of the big fat "jolly friar cookie jar" which
states on it "thou shalt not steal." The playful vision of the most
recent Pizza Hut commercial which has two friars exchanging a
"high five" as their paths crisscross on a snowy mountain on
their way up and down from their triple-decker cheese pizza.
Sorry, but you'd never see a Jesuit in that role there! The
Sherman-on-the-mount calendar and greeting cards, all capture

for me something, now that I look back, which started me off on my wild awesome adventure.

For as I look back I remember clearly as if yesterday. As an altar boy at Our Lady of the Snows Church in Floral Park, Queens, we had great priests! I don't have the horror stories other Catholics and the media relish reminding us of. My priests were good, dedicated, holy men. But I didn't want to be one of *them*.

FRIAR TUCK

It was after watching a fat, robed, bald man walk through a forest playfully, but with divine intention, with Robin Hood's motley crew, that I knew what I wanted to be. I saw Friar Tuck someone serving God, helping the poor and all people in trouble, simply by being their jolly friend.

Yes, this was the tool of the divine invitation for me . . . an infallible sign of the divine sense of humor, in calling a friar Tuck . . . in calling me . . . in calling all of us . . . the same experience the reader has embarked upon.

MYSTICAL SHERWOOD FOREST

Yes, it was *a friar's joy* that told me where I could find God! And how I could search, seek, live, play, and celebrate the rest of my life! We hope it has helped you find God too in some small way as you've journeyed with us through this mystical Sherwood Forest.

If you have learned what makes a friar tick; or what makes one happy. If you've gained any insight into what real joy is. If you have simply *enjoyed* the read, then it has all been worthwhile and we have accomplished our task! Praise God! Let us know if we have.

TABLE OF PLENTY

Please spread some of your own joy in the meantime! Don't be stingy with it! It will never run out! There's plenty to go around! There's a divine source flowing from the table of plenty. Remember the wonderful story of the widow and Elijah in the Old Testament book of Kings. How Elijah asked the widow to give him her last piece of bread, that the Lord would provide . . .

and "that her jar of flour from that day did not go empty, nor her jug of oil run dry, as the Lord had foretold" (1 Kings 17–16).

OUR FRIENDS

The friars minor recorded here pray that we can now call you our friends, for we have "revealed to you some of what the Father has shown us, spoken to us, done to or through us." Why? "So that our own joy may be in you, and that your own joy may be complete" (John 15:11). And if that happened in this *Fioretti*, then it truly has been *a friar's joy!*

WHY ELSE?

But that at the close of the second millennium that *you* may "tell the next generation that such is our God! Our God forever and always! It is the most high who leads us" (Psalm 48:15). And it is our great and glorious God who is the master giver of such joy that you have heard! To that God be all glory, now and forever and ever. Amen.

Afterthought

Joseph Stalin once said: "If I had ten men like Francis of Assisi, I could conquer the world!" Maybe you've met some of these men in this book who are working at it.

Mahatma Ghandi once said: "A small band of determined spirits fired by an unquenchable thirst for their mission, can alter the course of history!"

CAN A BOOK CHANGE THE WORLD?

Can a book change the world? No, but people can! I know some who are trying! Now, you've met them too! You know them! Let's do it!

At the end of the second millennium let's do it! Mother Teresa once described herself as a "small pencil in the hand of God who is writing a love letter to the world."

WAKE UP!

I like to think of us in similar ways, but also with this: I am a small pencil in the hand of God writing a word to twenty-first century dreamers and doers! Wake up, America! Wake up, everybody! Wake up, Catholics!

THREE KINDS OF PEOPLE

Somebody else once said that: "There are three kinds of people in this world: Those who *make* things happen! Those who *let* things happen! And those who say: *What Happened?*

Let's keep dreaming! Let's keep making God's dream come true! Let's do it. Let's *keep* doing it! Let's keep doing it *together!* And let's just *do* it! . . . in memory of him!

CAUTION!

He's risen! He's alive, and lives in us! And, we're bringing him with us into the third millennium! Wanna Come? Join us! But, be careful! Imagine a sign all lit up; envision a neon colored bright light flashing, flashing, flashing all lit up, giving the warning to the skeptical, to the cynical, to the cautious, to be careful. "The signs of the prophets are written on the subway walls and tenement halls." Be careful! The sign shouts ever so quietly:

JOY AT WORK!

Interactive Who's Who Contest

This is really a quiz to find out if you were paying attention! But really it's an invitation to you to give us some feedback . . . some friar foolery playback from our readers . . . some response and interaction.

This was not an ordinary book. Friars shared from the depths of their religious and personal experience. It kind of demands a response if it really worked! We want to give you the chance to respond.

INTERACT WITH US

We should like to offer you the opportunity to interact with us, to tell us what you have heard. Perhaps you can share how it has resonated in some way with your own personal experience of life, of God, of Church, of your own spiritual journey.

CONTEST RULES

Rule #1

Entrance fee: with a $1 entrance fee (may be larger if you *really* want to win!) for support of the *Friars Minor—Joy at Work*, check made to that title also please (for support of our Franciscan ministries).

Rule #2

Match the friars with their corresponding nicknames. Listing of names beginning on page 152; nicknames on page 113. Good Luck!

Rule #3

Tell us *which* story:

1 / *Touched* you most deeply, and *why*.

2 / Made you *laugh*.

3 / Was your overall *favorite*, and *why*.

Mail your entry to:

> *Franciscan Joy at Work*
> St. Anthony of Padua Friary
> P.O. Box 40
> Ho-Ho-Kus, N.J. 07423

Winners will be named and prizes awarded every feast of the Epiphany!

CAN A BOOK CHANGE THE WORLD?

NO, BUT PEOPLE CAN!

CAUTION: JOY AT WORK!

Franciscan Friars in This Book

JOHN ANGLIN, OFM: from South Boston, Mass. Ministry of Word, New England, from Annunciation Friary, Natick, Mass. Past: formation work, Buffalo, Bronx; Bolivian missions; pastoral work, Camden, N.J., St. Francis, N.Y.C.

MARTIN BEDNAR, OFM: from St. Petersburg, Fla. Ministry of Word, Florida, from Bellair Bluffs, Fla. Past: Bolivian missions, superior of mission; parish work, Bronx, Silver Spring, Md.

BRENNAN CONNOLLY, OFM: from Brighton, Mass. Ministry of Word, Metro, N.Y., from St. Anne's, Fairlawn, N.J. Past: formation in Callicoon; pastor, Elmwood Park, East Rutherford.

KEVIN CRONIN, OFM: from Bronx, Floral Park, Queens, N.Y.C. Ministry of Word, Metro, N.Y., from Ho-Ho-Kus, N.J. Past: pastoral team, Pompton Lakes, N.J. Vocation director. Associate pastor, St. Anthony Shrine, Boston.

MICHAEL DUFFY, OFM: from Ashland, N.H. Director, St. Francis Inn, Philadelphia. Past: pastoral work, East Rutherford, N.J., East Boston. Vocation director.

EDWARD FLANAGAN, OFM: from College Park, Md. Ministry of Word, Florida, from St. James of the Marches Friary, Bellair Bluffs, Fla. Past: formation, Callicoon; pastoral work, Ringwood, N.J. Marriage encounter.

JOHN KELLEHER, OFM: from Malden, Mass. Ministry of Word, Metro, N.Y. from Ho-Ho-Kus, N.J. Past: campus Ministry, St. Bonaventure University; parish, Little Falls, N.J.

DANIEL LANAHAN, OFM: from Metro, N.Y., Ministry of Word, Ho-Ho-Kus, N.J. Past: rector and professor, Christ the King

Seminary, East Aurora, N.Y., St. Bonaventure University. Co-founder Ministry of Word. Pastoral work, Wanaque, N.J., Long Beach Island, N.J.

CHARLES MILLER, OFM: from Gerard, Pa. Vice provincial, Holy Name Province, 96th Street, N.Y.C. Past: Pompton Lakes, N.J., Long Island Beach, N.J., Christhouse Retreat House, Lafayette, N.J. Brazilian Missions.

EMMET MURPHY, OFM: from Arlington, Mass. Ministry of Word, Metro, N.Y. from Ho-Ho-Kus, N.J. Past: pastoral work, Ringwood, N.J. Co-founder of St. Francis Inn, Philadelphia; work at St. Francis of Assisi, N.Y.C.

RONALD PECCI, OFM: from Brooklyn, N.Y., Creskill, N.J. Pastor, St. Rita/St. Patrick, Buffalo. Provincial Councillor, Vocation Director. Parish work, West Milford, N.J.

RODERIC PETRIE, OFM: from Canastota, N.Y.; Ministry of the Word, Florida. Past: high school teacher, Bishop Timon High School, Buffalo, N.Y.; Bishop Walsh High School, Olean, N.Y. Formation Work, Callicoon, N.Y. and Novitiate, Brookline, Mass. Cofounder St. Francis Inn, Philadelphia.

FRANCIS SMITH, OFM: from Philadelphia. Ministry of Word, Metro, N.Y. from Ho-Ho-Kus, N.J. Past: Bolivian missions; nursing, East Boston; pastoral work, Silver Spring, Md., Bronx.

THOMAS VIGLIOTTA, OFM: from Patchogue, Long Island. Ministry of Word, Florida. Past: Greenville, S.C. Franciscan Retreat Center, Tampa, Fla.

> "Blessed is that friar who finds all his joy in the words and deeds of our Lord, and uses them to help others to *Love God Gladly!*"—ST. FRANCIS

Serve the Lord with Gladness

Cry out with joy to the Lord all the earth!
Serve the Lord with gladness.
Come before the Most High singing for joy!

Know that the Most High, the Lord is God.
God made us. We belong to the Most High.
We are God's people, the sheep of his flock.

Go within God's gates giving thanks.
Enter God's courts with songs of praise!
Give thanks to God and bless God's name!

Indeed how good is the Lord.
Eternal God's merciful love.
God is faithful from age to age.

All glory be to the Most High and glorious God.

Now and forever and ever and ever. Amen.

PSALM 100

Take Courage, Dearest Brothers,
and
Rejoice in the Lord!
And do not be sad,
because you seem to be so few . . .
Because as the Lord has actually
shown me,
God is going to make us
into a very great multitude!
and spread us out in numbers
to the ends of the earth!

St. Francis of Assisi